FOR THE LOVE of PORTUGUESE FOOD

MILENA RODRIGUES

Copyright © 2017 Milena Rodrigues.

All rights reserved. No part of this book may be reproduced, stored, or transmitted by any means—whether auditory, graphic, mechanical, or electronic—without written permission of the author, except in the case of brief excerpts used in critical articles and reviews. Unauthorized reproduction of any part of this work is illegal and is punishable by law.

ISBN 978-0-692-89966-3

PRINTED AND BOUND IN THE U.S.A.

Table of Contents

Dedications iv
Obrigada!!! v
An Introduction To The Author viii

{
    Starters and Appetizers / Entradas e Petiscos 1
    Soups / Sopas 17
    Fish and Seafood / Peixe e Marisco 33
    Meat and Chicken / Carne e Galinha 53
    Other / Diversos 75
    Side Dishes / Acompanhamentos 83
    Desserts and Sweets / Sobremesas e Doces 99
    Bread / Pão 125
}

My Favorite Portugal 135
Index 139

Dedications

First, I would like to dedicate this book to the memory of my sister, Linda, who passed away on February 5, 2013, after a long battle with cancer. During her time on hospice, I finally took the first step towards my dream of writing a cookbook. That journey began with the creation of my Facebook page, where I started sharing my favorite Portuguese recipes. During that difficult time, when my sister was fighting through her last days, spending time on my page was a welcome distraction. Also, with her death, I realized that we often put things off for far too long thinking we have time, when we are actually just running out of time. At that moment, I decided to finally put my dream into motion.

Secondly, I want to dedicate this book to my two beautiful daughters, Maia and Leila. Just like me, they were born in the United States, started visiting Portugal at the age of one and return almost every summer. They are also are growing up eating and loving many traditional Portuguese foods, such as sardines and bacalhau, as I did. This book is my gift to them, so that one day they can cook the same meals that I prepared for them and my parents for me. Hopefully, many of these dishes will remind them of family, their childhood and our wonderful vacations in Portugal. I think it will.

Thirdly, I dedicate this book to all immigrants and their descendants who grew up eating Portuguese food. Compared to other types of cuisine, there are a limited number of Portuguese cookbooks written in English, and I hope to help fill that void. May these recipes help current and future generations continue the tradition of cooking and serving homemade Portuguese meals for themselves and their families.

Lastly, this cookbook is also for any non-Portuguese who have fallen in love with our cuisine and want to make and serve some of these meals at home themselves.

I am sharing here a little of what I have learned along the way about cooking some of our beloved Portuguese food. My dream is to keep the tradition of making hearty, homemade Portuguese meals alive; those foods we enjoyed so much with our families and will always treasure. May these recipes help many relive memories past triggered by the taste and smell of favorite dishes that we grew up with; those dishes that our loved ones, some living and some gone, prepared for us with so much love. Love was always a main ingredient and one of the reasons why Portuguese food always tasted so good, and still does.

Obrigada!!!

I would like to thank my family and friends who taught me a little something about Portuguese cooking, shared their favorite recipes and were always there to give me tips and answer questions. I could not have completed this book without them. I am so lucky to be surrounded by so many incredibly gifted cooks and bakers.

First, thank you to my mom, Encarnação, who taught me much of what I know about Portuguese cooking. Her cooking style is simple, yet delicious, and she is always just a phone call away. Like all Portuguese moms, she never had measurements to share, so I had to figure that part out all on my own.

Thank you to my sister, Laura, and brother-in law, Manuel, who are outstanding cooks and taught me much of what I know, especially related to preparing seafood dishes.

Also, thank you to my sister, Linda, in heaven. She was an amazing cook and another great resource. So many times, I picked up the phone and called her in the middle of cooking to clarify how to make a certain dish. Unfortunately, this is no longer possible since she is now gone. I miss her dearly.

Thank you to the best baker I know, my Tia Lourdes. She makes the most incredible desserts and shared some of her favorite recipes with me. She too, also taught me many things about baking Portuguese goodies, including many handy tips.

Thank you to my sister-in-law, Alice, and mother-in-law, Patrocinia, who taught me how to make fresh cheese, something that I have loved since a child. Alice also taught me how to make other favorites, including Folar de Chaves and Cavacas.

Thank you to my husband for continually encouraging me. He is my biggest fan, as well as my biggest critic and my main taste tester. I can always count on him for his honest opinion. He has undoubtedly made me a better cook and one of the main reasons I cook with love.

A special thank you to my friend, Idalecia André, who helped me with recipes for Broa and Folar de Páscoa. I wanted to make these just the way they were made in our region of Portugal. She was kind enough to share her recipes with me and answer all of my questions.

A very special heartfelt thank you to two friends who always supported me on this journey and motivated me with their words of encouragement throughout the way. Thank you Erin Silva and Ellie Velosa Camarão! I appreciate both of you more than you know!

Thank you to all taste testers: Nelson Rodrigues, Andrea Grilo, Miguel Evangelista, Juraci Capataz, Maia Rodrigues and Leila Rodrigues.

Thank you to my recipe testers: Erin Silva, Ellie Velosa Camarão, Ryan Pereira and Hilaria Sousa.

Thank you to my friends who helped edit and proofread my manuscript: Erin Silva, Maria Igrejas Matos, Beatriz Oliveira and Dorinda Fidalgo-Ribeiro.

I also must thank all of my Facebook followers, many of whom expressed their appreciation for sharing my recipes and provided much encouragement throughout the last few years. My followers have truly been a source of motivation and inspiration since the beginning.

An Introduction To The Author

I am an American-born Portuguese girl with a love of life, food and just about anything Portuguese. I am not a chef and never had any professional training in cooking. I just simply enjoy cooking some good homemade food for my loved ones. Everything I know, I learned from my family and friends or learned on my own as I went along. My style of cooking is similar to that of my mom's. She uses simple ingredients that most of us tend to always have at home such as garlic, onions, tomatoes, olive oil, wine, beer, bay leaves, potatoes, etc. These ingredients are used in many of my recipes over and over again.

I grew up in the United States in a home where Portuguese was the primary language spoken, and I spoke Portuguese before I spoke English. I grew up in a home where my mother made most of my clothes when I was a child and where my dad salted his own cod and hung it out on the clothesline to dry. Also, in our house, we never ever ate soup out of a can. Our soups were always homemade with love. We also ate our fish whole with the heads still on and bones still in them. My family kept many of the Portuguese traditions alive, and for that, I am grateful. I cannot imagine growing up any other way. My heritage is a vital part of whom I am and has shaped me into the person I am today.

My parents immigrated to the U.S. with my two sisters in 1966 from Figueira da Foz, Portugal to Gloucester, Massachusetts. Three years later, I was born. I was a bit of a surprise, as my sisters were 14 and 16 years old at the time. My parents were certainly not planning on having any more children, but then I came along. Because my dad was a fisherman, my parents eventually moved from Gloucester to New Bedford, which had a larger fishing port. My dad's fishing career began at a very young age in Portugal. At the age of 14, he went on his first cod fishing trip traveling all the way from Portugal to the waters of Newfoundland. When my dad was not fishing for cod, he was fishing for sardines out of the port of Figueira da Foz. For generations, my family's livelihood was fishing. Therefore, salt cod and sardines were a staple in my parents' home, and I continue the tradition in my own home today.

My first trip to Portugal was at the young age of one, when I had barely just started walking. After that, I visited almost every summer, even in the years my parents did not go. I honestly have lost count of how many times I have been there. My parents often sent me to stay with my sister, who moved back after getting married. I fell in love with Portugal at a very young age – the people, the food and the lifestyle and always looked forward to the summers there. As a young adult, my summers were filled with fun and adventures with friends: hopping into taxis, buses and trains to explore the country from North to South, and never did I feel unsafe. Today, I continue to vacation in Portugal almost every summer with my husband and two daughters, who love Portugal as much as I do.

The idea to write a cookbook came to me many years ago when I started searching for a Portuguese cookbook, written in English, to donate as an auction item for a Chinese raffle. I searched the internet and bookstores, but found very few options available. At that point, I realized that I wanted to write a Portuguese cookbook in English to help fill this void and help promote the Portuguese cuisine and culture that I love so much. Also, I wanted to write a cookbook as a gift to my daughters, so that they could carry on the tradition of making Portuguese food at home for themselves and someday for their own families.

Starters and Appetizers / Entradas e Petiscos

- Littleneck Clams with Garlic and Wine Sauce / Ameijoas à Bulhão Pato
- Codfish Cakes / Pasteis de Bacalhau
- Fresh Cheese / Queijo Fresco
- Spanish Style Littleneck Clams / Ameijoas à Espanhola
- Shrimp Mozambique / Camarão à Moçambique
- Tuna Pate / Patê de Atum
- Farinheira Sausage with Scrambled Eggs / Farinheira com Ovos Mexidos
- Tempura Green Beans / Peixinhos da Horta

In this section, I would like to share recipes for some of the most loved Portuguese appetizers. Many of these have been a favorite of mine since I was a small child, including Codfish Cakes, Littleneck Clams with Garlic / Wine Sauce and Fresh Cheese. Each of these brings back special memories of growing up in a Portuguese home, as well as my summers in Portugal. When vacationing in Portugal, Fresh Cheese was often a part of breakfast, accompanied with some fresh bread. Also, when going out to dinner with my parents, I often ordered Littleneck Clams with Garlic / Wine Sauce as my meal with a side of homemade fries. Shrimp Mozambique, although not seen on menus in the restaurants in Portugal, is quite popular in Portuguese communities in the U.S., and few things taste better with a fresh Papo Seco (Portuguese bread roll). What's better than a Papo Seco to soak up that sauce?

Littleneck Clams with Garlic and Wine Sauce / Ameijoas à Bulhão Pato

Makes 6 to 8 servings

5 pounds fresh small littleneck clams
⅓ cup olive oil
5 garlic cloves, minced

½ cup white wine
3 tablespoons parsley or cilantro, chopped

Soak clams in water and scrub them to clean any particles or grit from the outside surface. Lift clams out of water into another bowl of clean water. Do not simply dump clams into the second bowl, as you will also dump sand along with clams. Do this a couple of times to ensure that the sand has been removed. Note: Soak fresh clams in water with salt overnight to encourage them to squirt some of the sand out.

In a large frying pan or saucepan, heat olive oil and add garlic. Sauté garlic for 1 to 2 minutes, being very careful not to burn. Add wine and bring to a simmering boil.

Add littleneck clams, cover pan and cook on medium - high heat until all clams open: approximately 5-8 minutes depending on the size of clams. Discard any clams that do not open. Add parsley / cilantro and stir. Remove clams from pan and place in a serving dish.

After removing clams, allow sauce to simmer in pan for 2-3 minutes on medium heat. Then pour sauce over littleneck clams in the serving dish. Garnish with additional chopped parsley / cilantro and lemon wedges.

Growing up in the house of a fisherman, Codfish Cakes were a staple at our house. My dad often came home with fresh cod, which he would then salt himself. After the cod was salted for some time, it was hung on the clothesline to dry: a vivid memory that will live in my mind forever.

I am extremely proud to come from a family of fisherman. Both of my grandfathers were also fisherman. What my grandfathers, dad and even uncles endured at sea and away from home is beyond anything that many of us have experienced. I will always admire my ancestors for their bravery. My dad went on his first cod fishing trip at the age of 14 and completed over 20 trips during his lifetime. This meant leaving the family for six months at a time and traveling thousands of miles to the waters off Newfoundland and Greenland. When he was not fishing for cod, he was fishing for sardines out of Figueira da Foz. No wonder cod and sardines are among my favorite Portuguese foods. It's in my blood!

Codfish Cakes / Pasteis de Bacalhau

Makes 18 to 24 codfish cakes

1 pound salted cod
4 medium russet potatoes (approximately 1 pound), peeled and cubed
1 onion, finely chopped

2 large eggs
1 handful fresh flat-leaf parsley, finely chopped
Salt, pepper and garlic powder to taste
Vegetable oil

....

Desalt cod ahead of time by soaking in a large bowl of cold water, making sure to cover cod completely, for at least 24 hours and up to 48 hours (depending on thickness of cod). Refrigerate and change water approximately every six hours. The first change of water should be about two hours after initial soaking.

Boil cod for approximately 8 to 10 minutes or until cooked. Drain water and set aside. Allow to cool. Flake and shred cod with your hands after removing skin and bones.

Boil potatoes until tender. Drain potatoes and place in a bowl. Mash potatoes with a potato masher until smooth.

Add flaked cod, onion, eggs and parsley to mashed potatoes and blend well with a wooden spoon. Season with salt, pepper and garlic powder. You may or may not need to add salt depending on how salty cod is.

With a tablespoon, scoop up a heaping spoon of cod / potato mixture and form into the shape of an egg with hands or using two tablespoons.

In the meantime, heat oil in a large frying pan. Add enough oil so that it comes approximately ½" up the side of the pan. When oil is hot, fry codfish cakes until they are a golden brown, turning them a few times to ensure that they fry all over.

Remove codfish cakes with a slotted spoon or tongs and place on a plate lined with paper towels to soak up the oil. Serve at room temperature or cold.

Fresh cheese has been a long-time favorite of mine. However, I learned how to make it only just a few years ago from my sister-in-law, Alice, and mother-in-law, Patrocinia. My husband's family is from the Serra da Estrela region and were farmers and cheese-makers, so who better to learn from than them? The traditional way of making fresh cheese in their region involves pressing the cheese with two hands after it is drained and put in the molds. This process helps to get much of the liquid whey out of the cheese before it is even refrigerated. I like to continue this tradition when making my fresh cheese. Fresh cheese that is less watery lasts longer, as it does not sour as quickly. Also, it retains it original size better compared to cheese that is left with too much liquid. However, you can drain and / or press the cheese as much or as little as you want to suit your taste.

Fresh Cheese / Queijo Fresco

Makes 10 to 12 servings

2 gallons whole milk
2 to 3 tablespoons salt

2 teaspoons rennet powder

....

Preheat oven to 250 degrees F. As soon as preheated, turn off the oven.

Pour milk into a large stockpot and add salt. Warm milk on the stovetop on medium heat until lukewarm, stirring constantly with a wooden spoon. Once milk is lukewarm, immediately remove from heat. Be sure to not overheat or allow to boil.

In a small dish, add approximately ⅓ cup of warmed milk and rennet powder. Stir until rennet powder is completely dissolved and then pour back into stockpot. Stir well to incorporate dissolved rennet evenly throughout.

Cover stockpot containing warmed milk and place into the oven. Be sure the oven is no longer on, but is warm after having been preheated. Leave milk in the oven until it coagulates and has the appearance of yogurt - approximately 1-2 hours.

Once milk has coagulated, remove from oven. Cut through coagulated milk with a knife, making horizontal and vertical cuts throughout, into a crisscross pattern. Leave uncovered for approximately 20 minutes to allow whey (liquid) to separate from milk curds.

Place a cheesecloth or very thin dishcloth in large colander / strainer on top of large bowl / pan and set in the sink. Pour or spoon coagulated milk into colander and allow to drain for approximately 20 minutes. After much of whey has drained, grab ends of cheesecloth, bringing the ends together and squeezing into a ball to drain more liquid from the milk curds.

Place drained milk curds in a cheese mold on a flat plate. Set a clean cheesecloth / dishcloth on top of cheese in the mold and press firmly with your hands to squeeze out more of the whey. To drain the liquid out of the plate, carefully hold the cheese mold and tilt the plate into the sink. Repeat the process of pressing cheese with your hands several times to get most of liquid out of cheese. Exactly how much liquid you want to squeeze out is a matter of preference, depending on whether you like a more or less watery cheese.

When the majority of liquid has been removed from cheese, sprinkle a little salt on top of both sides and then place the cheese mold in the refrigerator overnight. Check on it occasionally and discard any additional liquid that drains out into the plate.

To serve, remove cheese from the mold and carefully place on a serving dish. Serve with fresh Portuguese "papo secos" and / or "pimenta moida" . The cheese should last approximately five days in the refrigerator.

NOTE: Makes 2 medium to large cheeses. Cheese molds can be purchased at Portuguese Markets or online. The mold should be open on the top and bottom and have holes all around the sides. The rennet powder can also be purchased at a Portuguese market or even some supermarkets.

Spanish Style Littleneck Clams / Ameijoas à Espanhola

Makes 6 to 8 servings

3½ to 4 pounds of fresh, small littleneck clams
⅓ cup olive oil
3 onions, thinly sliced crosswise
3 garlic cloves, minced
1 bay leaf
4 tomatoes, cubed
1 red pepper, cut into thin 1" slices

½ cup white wine
½ cup water
Salt and pepper to taste
Hot sauce (optional)
1 sprig parsley, chopped
Lemon juice

....

Soak clams in water and scrub them to clean any particles or grit from the outside surface. Lift clams out of water into another bowl of clean water. Do not simply dump clams into the second bowl, as you will also dump sand along with the clams. Do this a couple of times to ensure that the sand has been removed. Note: Soak fresh clams in water with salt overnight to encourage them to squirt some of the sand out.

Heat olive oil and add onions, garlic and bay leaf. Sauté until onions become translucent. Add tomatoes and red pepper slices. Allow to simmer covered until tomatoes and peppers are cooked. Add wine and water. Add salt and pepper to taste.

If you like this dish spicy, add a couple of dashes of hot sauce. Bring to a boil and allow to simmer for an additional five minutes. Add littlenecks and cover. When littleneck shells open, remove lid, add chopped parsley, mix well and allow to simmer a few additional minutes uncovered. Squeeze a little lemon juice over littlenecks and serve.

Shrimp Mozambique / Camarão à Moçambique

Makes 4 servings

¼ cup olive oil
6 cloves garlic, minced
1 to 1½ pounds of shrimp
Juice from 1 lemon
1½ packets of Sazón Goya con Azafran seasoning

½ cup beer
1 tablespoon butter
A few dashes piri piri / hot sauce
1 tablespoon parsley, chopped

....

Heat olive oil in a large frying pan, and then add garlic. Sauté garlic on medium heat for approximately one minute (making sure not to burn). Add shrimp and bring to a simmer. Add lemon juice and Goya seasoning. Stir well so that shrimp is evenly coated.

Next, add beer, butter and a few dashes of hot sauce. Bring to a boil on high heat and then reduce heat to medium. Simmer until shrimp is cooked, stirring occasionally.

When cooked, remove shrimp from the frying pan to allow sauce to reduce and thicken. When it has thickened, pour sauce over shrimp, squeeze a little more lemon juice over shrimp and toss chopped fresh parsley on top as well. Serve with fresh "Papo Secos" (Portuguese bread rolls) to soak up sauce.

Tuna Pate is a popular starter in Portugal and is typically served with small, toasty bread. It is a very quick and easy appetizer to make. I like to serve it at parties as an appetizer.

Tuna Pate / Patê de Atum

Makes 24 – 30 servings

2 cans (4.2 ounces) Portuguese tuna, drained and flaked
1 medium onion, chopped
4 tablespoons mayonnaise
1 tablespoon fresh parsley, chopped
2 teaspoons vinegar
Salt and pepper to taste
Small toasted bread

....

Drain tuna well. Add onion, mayonnaise, parsley, vinegar, salt and pepper into a food processor or blender. Chop until smooth. Place in a serving bowl, cover and refrigerate for a minimum of one hour.

Serve with small, dry, crunchy toasts.

I like to call Farinheira, "the other Portuguese sausage", because it is not so recognized as linguiça, chouriço or morcela. Farinheira is made with flour, pork fat and seasonings. It is indeed a very flavorful sausage. Here is a popular appetizer made with farinheira. This sausage is also very popular in the Portuguese cozido.

Farinheira Sausage with Scrambled Eggs / Farinheira com Ovos Mexidos

Makes 4 servings

1 farinheira sausage
6 large eggs
Salt and pepper to taste

½ cup olive oil
1 sprig parsley, chopped

Remove casing from farinheira sausage and break its contents into smaller bite sized pieces.

In a mixing bowl, whisk eggs until well blended. Add salt and pepper to taste. The farinheira is already quite salty, so little or no salt is needed.

Heat olive oil in a large frying pan. Add farinheira bits into the frying pan and fry them up a little allowing to brown only slightly.

Add whisked eggs into the frying pan and stir with a wooden spoon so that the farinheira bits and eggs are well blended. Fry until eggs are cooked just as you would do when making scrambled eggs.

Garnish with fresh chopped parsley.

NOTE: Alheira can also be used in place of farinheira.

We often associate tempura with Japan. However, it was the Portuguese who taught the Japanese about tempura. Literally translated, "Peixinhos da Horta" means Little Garden Fish. The name comes from the fact that these Tempura Green Beans look like fried fish. I never had these growing up, but they were popular with my husband's family. In fact, I only had these for the first time after I met my husband, who is from the Serra da Estrela region of Portugal. Like chips, once you start eating these, you can't stop!

Tempura Green Beans / Peixinhos da Horta

Makes 4 to 6 servings

1 pound fresh green beans
1 cup all-purpose flour
1 cup water

3 large eggs
Salt and pepper to taste
2 cups vegetable or canola oil

After washing and snipping ends of green beans, cook them in boiling water seasoned with a little salt for approximately 5-8 minutes. Be sure not to overcook green beans.

Drain green beans and dry them off in a paper towel.

In a bowl, combine flour and water. The mixture should not be too liquidy or too thick. Next, add eggs and mix well with fork / whisk until a smooth batter forms. Add salt and pepper to taste.

Heat oil in large frying pan. When oil is ready, reduce to medium heat. Dip beans in batter, a few at a time, and fry until golden brown. When they are ready, remove green beans from frying pan using a slotted spoon. Place on a dish lined with a paper towel to absorb some of oil.

Peixinhos da Horta can be served hot or cold.

Soups / Sopas

- Portuguese Green Soup / Caldo Verde
- Pureed Vegetable Soup / Sopa de Creme de Legumes
- Cabbage Soup / Sopa de Repolho
- Kale Soup with Beans / Sopa de Couves com Feijão
- Chicken Soup / Canja
- Pureed Red Kidney Bean Soup / Sopa de Feijão Encarnado
- Green Bean Soup / Sopa de Feijão Verde
- Leek Soup / Sopa de Alho Francês

Growing up Portuguese meant eating hearty, homemade soups. My mom often made a large pot of soup, which lasted for days. Soup was her thing. Today, I make many of the same soups my mom made. I consider my soup a success if it comes out tasting like hers!

The most recognized Portuguese soup is Caldo Verde, which originated in Northern Portugal. This soup is made with just a few simple ingredients and tastes delicious. The traditional version of Caldo Verde is made with a green called "couve galega" which can be found in Portugal and the Galicia region of Spain. In the United States, Collard Greens are the closest thing to this type of green. However, there are some people that do use kale when making this soup. Also, for this soup, the greens are traditionally cut very thin ("chiffonade" style).

Portuguese Green Soup / Caldo Verde

Makes 8 to 10 servings

- 4 cups collard greens / kale (approx. 1.25 pound bunch), cut into very thin strips
- 4 to 5 quarts water
- 8 to 10 medium potatoes, peeled and cut into quarters
- 1 medium onion, peeled and cut in half
- 3 garlic cloves, peeled and whole
- 2 tablespoons olive oil
- Salt and pepper to taste
- ½ pound chouriço or linguiça, sliced crosswise into ¼" slices

....

Wash collard greens / kale well and remove the thick stalks. To slice greens, take a few leaves at a time and roll them up tightly. Slice greens into very thin strips and then cut the thin strips into shorter strips if they are too long.

In a large stockpot, bring water to a boil. Add potatoes, onion, garlic, olive oil, salt and pepper.

Cover and boil gently over medium heat for 30 / 40 minutes or until potatoes are tender. Remove potatoes, onion and garlic and puree in blender and then return pureed vegetables to pot or use a hand blender to puree right in stockpot.

Next, add sliced linguiça / chouriço to soup. Once soup starts to boil again, add collard greens / kale. Simmer until collard greens / kale are cooked, leaving the pot covered. Skim off any sausage fat that floats to the surface of soup and discard. Once collard greens / kale are cooked, allow to simmer a bit without the cover to allow soup to thicken a bit and to your liking.

Tip: You may boil the sliced collard greens / kale in a separate pot before adding it to the soup if you prefer a whiter broth in your Caldo Verde. Also, if you want a thicker soup, you can add more potatoes or less potatoes for a lighter soup. Also, it is traditional to drizzle the soup with a little olive oil once plated.

A very popular soup served in Portugal is Pureed Vegetable Soup. This soup is a medley of vegetables that are pureed into a smooth, creamy consistency. Both adults and kids love this soup, making it a good way to get your children to eat some healthy vegetables. My girls love it!

Pureed Vegetable Soup / Sopa de Creme de Legumes

Makes 8 to 10 servings

2 leeks, rinsed and sliced into small pieces
5 quarts water
2 chicken bouillon cubes
5 potatoes, peeled and cut in half or cubed
2 zucchini, peeled, seeded and cubed
4 carrots, peeled and cut into smaller pieces

1 onion, peeled and whole
2 garlic cloves, peeled and whole
1 turnip, peeled and cut in half
2 tablespoons olive oil
2 cups cabbage, cut into bite-sized pieces
Salt to taste

Remove roots from leeks. Cut leeks lengthwise and rinse well under running water to remove any soil. Cut white portion of leeks into smaller pieces and discard the greener portion or save for another purpose.

In a large stockpot, add water and bouillon cubes. Bring to a boil. Add potatoes, zucchini, carrots, onion, garlic, leeks, turnip and olive oil. Reduce heat to medium and cook covered for approximately 40 minutes or until all vegetables are cooked.

Once cooked and tender, puree vegetables in a blender / food processor and return to pot, or use a hand blender to puree right in stockpot. Cover and bring to a boil. Add salt to taste.

Add cabbage and cook covered on medium heat until cabbage is cooked. Remove cover and simmer until soup reaches desired thickness.

For me, few things are more comforting than a good bowl of homemade soup. This one happens to be one of my favorites. Sopa de Repolho is hearty, filling and delicious!

Cabbage Soup / Sopa de Repolho

Makes 8 to 10 servings

4 to 5 quarts water
5 medium potatoes, peeled and cut into quarters
4 large carrots, peeled and cut in half
1 medium onion, peeled and cut in half
2 garlic cloves, peeled and whole
⅓ pound piece linguiça

1 tablespoon olive oil
1 beef bouillon cube (optional)
Salt to taste
½ medium-sized cabbage
1 can (15 ounces) cannellini beans
1 cup macaroni

....

Bring water to a boil in a large stockpot. Add potatoes, carrots, onion, garlic, linguiça, olive oil, beef bouillon and salt to taste. Reduce heat to medium until potatoes and carrots are cooked and tender.

Once cooked and tender, puree vegetables in a blender / food processor and return to pot, or use a hand blender to puree right in stockpot. (If using a hand blender, be sure to remove linguiça first).

Add cabbage, bring to a boil with cover on and then lower heat to a simmer for approximately 30 minutes. Next, add macaroni and beans. Bring the pan to a boil again and then reduce heat. Let soup simmer on low with cover on until macaroni is cooked. If you want a thicker soup, you can let it simmer without the lid on until desired thickness is reached.

Also instead of linguiça, you can use other meats, such as a couple of beef ribs. You can also leave the meats out altogether, especially if you use the beef bouillon.

There are many delicious Portuguese soups to choose from. Here's one of the most recognized. Some simply call it Portuguese Soup. I like call it Portuguese Kale and Bean soup, not to be confused with Portuguese Green Soup or Caldo Verde, which is a completely different soup altogether.

In my recipe, I like to puree the potatoes, onions, garlic, etc. while some recipes do not puree the vegetables and leave the potatoes cubed. Also, I like to add in a turnip or two and some carrots. These are optional. No matter which way you make it, it's very hearty and tasty!

Kale Soup with Beans / Sopa de Couves com Feijão

Makes 8 to 10 servings

4 to 5 quarts water
5 medium potatoes, peeled and cut in quarters
1 medium onion, peeled and cut in half
2 garlic cloves, peeled and whole
2 turnips, peeled and cut in quarters
1 tablespoon olive oil
Salt to taste

3 carrots, peeled and cut into ¼" rounds
1 large bunch of kale or collard greens, stemmed and roughly chopped
8 ounces linguiça or chouriço, sliced ¼" thick
1 can (15.5 ounces) red kidney beans, rinsed and drained
1 cup elbow macaroni

In a large stockpot, bring water to a boil. Add potatoes, onion, garlic, turnips, olive oil and salt. Cook on medium heat with cover. When vegetables are cooked and tender, puree them in a blender and return to pot or use a hand blender to puree right in stockpot.

Bring to a boil once again. Add carrots, kale / collard greens and linguiça / chouriço. Once kale / collard greens and carrots are almost cooked, add beans and macaroni. Allow to simmer uncovered until beans and macaroni are cooked.

Note: You may also cook some beans with the vegetables and include in the puree.

Chicken Soup / Canja

Makes 8 to 10 servings

5 quarts water
3 pound whole chicken
1 medium onion, peeled and whole
3 garlic cloves, peeled and whole

3 chicken bouillon cubes
1 cup orzo pasta
3 or 4 eggs
Pepper to taste

....

In a large stockpot, add water, chicken, onion, garlic and bouillon cubes. Bring to a boil and then reduce to a simmer, leaving the pot partially covered. Skim and discard foam / fat that floats to the top.

When chicken is cooked, carefully remove from pot and set aside to cool. In the meantime, bring the pot to a boil again and add orzo pasta, partially covering pot and reducing to a simmer.

When chicken is cool enough to handle, remove meat, discard skin and bones and cut chicken into bite-size pieces / strips. Return chicken strips / pieces to the pot. When orzo is almost cooked, crack a few eggs and drop right into soup. Allow to simmer uncovered until eggs and pasta are fully cooked. Add pepper to taste. Remove boiled onion from soup before serving.

Sliced / chopped carrots may also be added to this soup and rice can be substituted for the orzo, as well as any other small pasta.

Pureed Red Kidney Bean Soup / Sopa de Feijão Encarnado

Makes 8 to 10 servings

5 quarts water
1 medium onion, peeled and cut in half
2 garlic cloves, peeled and whole
3 carrots, peeled and cut into small pieces
1 tablespoon olive oil

⅓ pound piece linguiça
2 cans (15 ounces) red kidney beans, drained and rinsed
¾ cup Acini di Pepe pasta
Salt to taste

Bring water to a boil in a large stockpot. Add onion, garlic, carrots, olive oil and linguiça. Season with salt to taste and cook covered until vegetables are tender.

Add kidney beans to the stockpot and simmer covered for another 20 minutes. Remove all vegetables (including beans), puree with a blender and return to pot or use a hand blender to puree right in stockpot. If using a hand blender, be sure to remove the linguiça, as this should not be pureed.

Once vegetables are pureed, bring them to a boil in the stockpot and add pasta. Let soup simmer on medium heat covered until pasta is cooked. In the last 10 minutes, reduce heat and remove cover until soup reaches a medium thickness. This soup should not be too watery, nor too thick. If at any time the soup becomes too thick, simply add a little more water and allow to simmer a little longer.

There are many variations to this soup. Some people add cabbage after the other vegetables are pureed and others use macaroni for the pasta. Also, some include potatoes and / or turnips in this soup. In addition, the linguiça can be omitted from the recipe. Also, you do not need to puree all of the beans. Some can be left whole if you so choose.

Green Bean Soup / Sopa de Feijão Verde

Makes 8 to 10 servings

4 to 5 quarts water
5 medium potatoes, peeled and cut in half
1 medium onion, peeled and whole
2 garlic cloves, peeled and whole
5 medium tomatoes (2 cut in half to be pureed and 3 peeled and cut into quarters)
5 large carrots, peeled (3 cut in half and 2 sliced crosswise)
1 tablespoon olive oil
¼ pound piece linguiça
1½ pounds green beans, sliced crosswise diagonally or 1½ pounds frozen French sliced green beans
Salt and pepper to taste

....

Bring water to a boil in a large stock pot and add salt and pepper to taste.

Add potatoes, onion, garlic, halved tomatoes, halved carrots, olive oil and linguiça. (NOTE: Set carrots that were sliced crosswise and tomatoes that were cut in quarters aside and save for later).

Cover and allow to cook at low / medium heat until potatoes, carrots and tomatoes are cooked and tender.

Remove all cooked vegetables and puree in a blender or food processor. Leave the linguiça in the pot. You can also use a hand blender and blend right in the pot. Just be sure to remove the linguiça before doing so.

Once vegetables are pureed, bring to a boil. Add green beans, sliced carrots and quartered tomatoes and bring to a boil again.

Lower the heat and allow green beans, carrots and tomatoes to cook for approximately 45 minutes with the lid on or until all veggies just added are cooked.

Remove the lid and let soup simmer on low until soup starts to thicken a bit. The soup should not be too watery. It becomes much more flavorful if simmers uncovered on the stove for a while and is allowed to thicken.

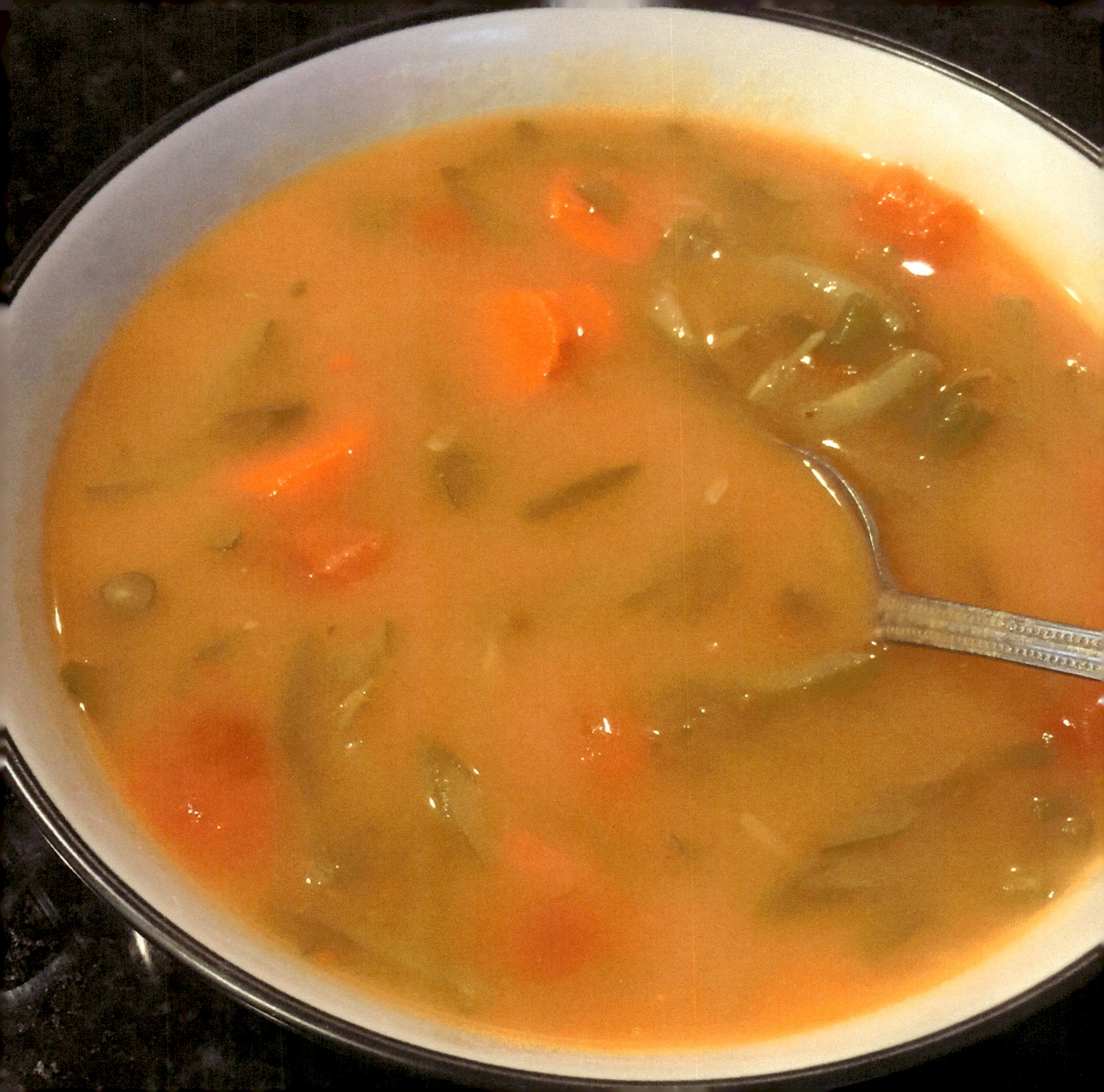

Leek Soup / Sopa de Alho Francês

Makes 8 to 10 servings

3 large leeks, rinsed and sliced into small pieces
5 quarts water
6 to 8 medium potatoes, peeled and cubed
1 medium onion, peeled and whole

3 garlic cloves, peeled and whole
5 carrots, peeled and cut into small pieces
⅓ cup olive oil
Salt to taste

....

Remove root end of leeks and discard. Cut lower, white portions, slice in half and wash well to remove any soil. Set aside.

Wash remaining, green portion of leeks to remove any soil and chop into small, rectangular pieces. Set aside.

Bring water to a boil in a large stockpot. Add potatoes, white portion of leeks, onion, garlic and carrots. Season with salt and cook covered until vegetables are tender (approximately 30 mins). When vegetables are tender, remove vegetables, puree with a blender and return to pot or use a hand blender right in pot.

In the meantime, in a frying pan, sauté chopped green portion of leeks in olive oil for about 5 minutes.

Add sautéed leeks to pureed vegetables in the soup pot after bringing the pot to a boil. Reduce heat and allow to simmer uncovered on low medium heat for approximately 30 minutes or until soup reaches a consistency that is not too watery, nor too thick.

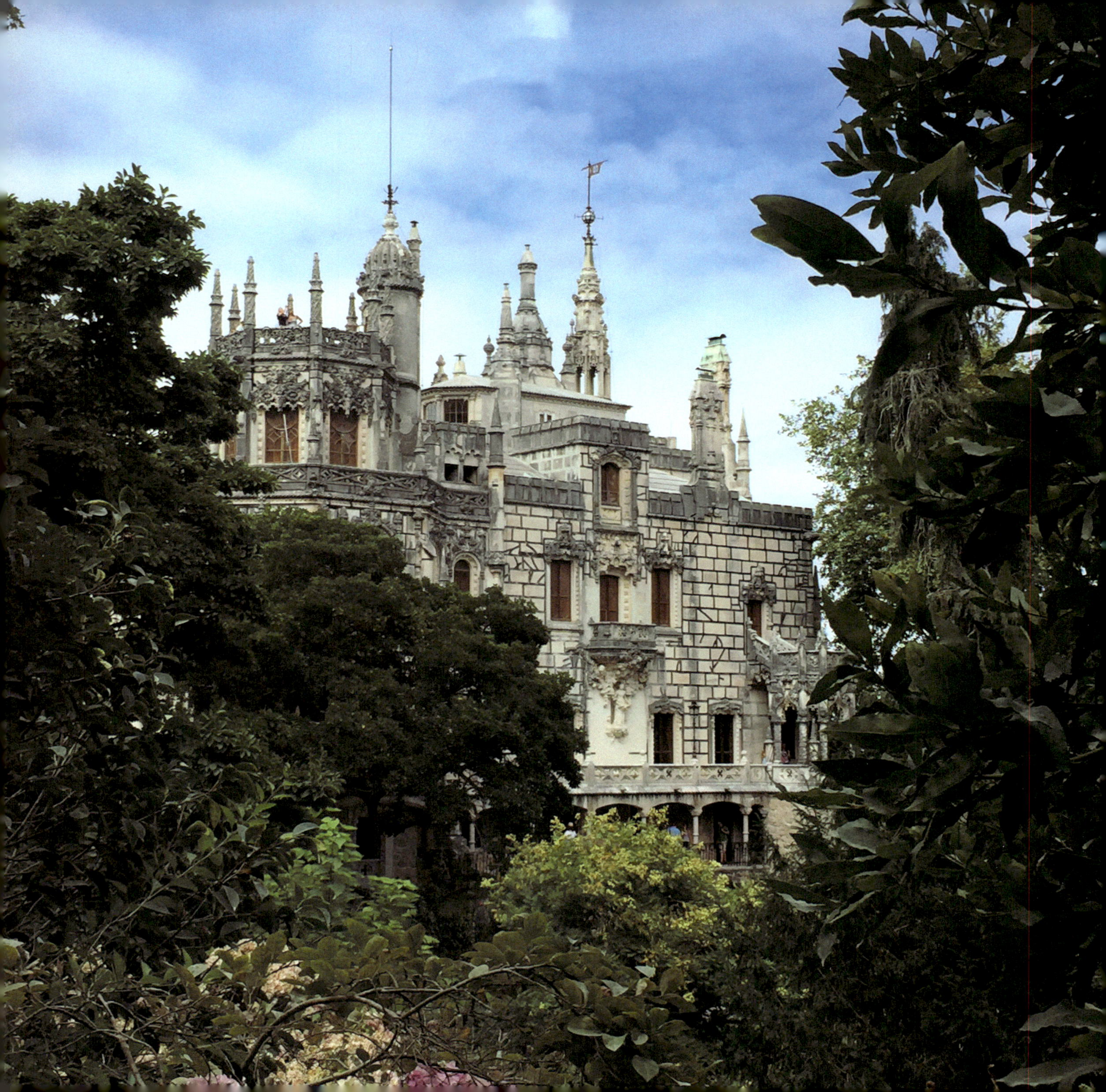

Fish and Seafood / Peixe e Marisco

- Grilled Sardines / Sardinhas Assadas
- Fried Salted Cod with Sautéed Onions / Bacalhau Frito com Cebolada
- Salted Cod Gomes de Sá Style / Bacalhau à Gomes de Sá
- Salted Cod with Eggs and Fries / Bacalhau à Brás
- Salted Cod Lagareiro Style / Bacalhau à Lagareiro
- Salted Cod with Heavy Cream / Bacalhau com Natas
- Stewed Squid with Potatoes / Lulas Guisadas com Batatas
- Stewed Squid with Rice / Lulas Guisadas com Arroz
- Baked Fish with Potatoes / Peixe Assado com Batatas
- Monkfish Stew / Caldeirada de Tamboril
- Small Fried Sardines with Escabeche Sauce / Petinga Frita com Molho Escabeche
- Seafood Macaroni / Massada de Marisco

Growing up in the home of a fisherman meant that we ate seafood very often. Frequently on the menu were salted cod, sardines, whiting, lobster, crab, squid and almost anything the sea had to offer. I loved them all. We were lucky to get all of our seafood fresh and for free when my dad was fishing. Growing up, one of my favorite dishes was Bacalhau à Gomes de Sá, and it still is today. Also, I have always loved sardines and simple boiled whiting with potatoes and green beans, which my parents served regularly. The love of seafood continues into the newer generations in our family. My oldest daughter's favorite food is grilled sardines. Coincidentally, or not, sardines have always been my mom's favorite food too. I guess it's in the genes.

Grilled Sardines / Sardinhas Assadas

Frozen sardines (3 to 4 per person)
Sea salt to taste

....

Allow sardines to thaw and then rinse under cold running water, removing any ice still on them. Place in a shallow baking dish or tray and season with coarse sea salt, making sure to coat them well on both sides.

Set sardines aside for 30 to 60 minutes in the salt. When ready, place sardines on a very hot grill, preferably charcoal. Allow to grill approximately 3-6 minutes on each side or until they start turning a golden color. If the grill starts to fire up too much due to the oil dripping from the sardines, simply sprinkle a little water on the flames. Serve sardines with boiled, salted potatoes with skin on, a fresh salad, Portuguese corn bread and grilled peppers.

NOTE: Frozen sardines imported from Portugal can be purchased at local Portuguese markets, if you have them in your area. They are sold in bags and include approximately 8 per bag. You can estimate 3 to 4 sardines per person on average to determine how many bags you need to purchase. The sardines are grilled whole, with heads and bones. They are eaten by hand and you must be very careful not to swallow any of the bones. If you do, eat a piece of bread and that should take care of it.

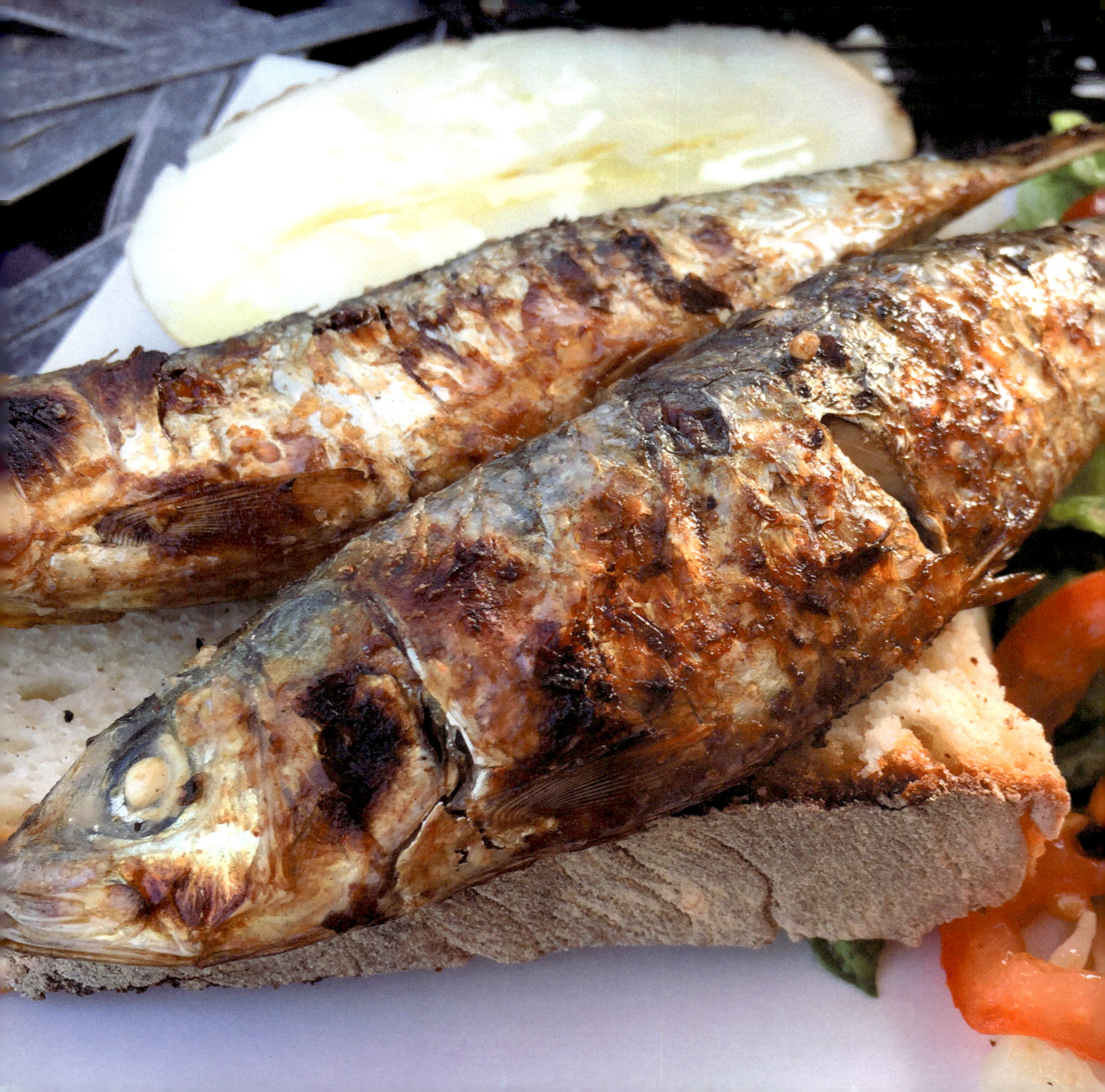

My dad was a cod fisherman for many years, completing a total of 23 trips, with his first trip at the young age of 14. Fishing for cod required leaving the family for 6 months at a time and travelling all the way from Portugal to the Grand Banks. I am lucky to have a register with all of his cod fishing trips logged. During his first few trips, my paternal grandfather was also part of the crew. Both were very hardworking, brave men indeed. My grandfather received a medal of honor for saving an entire ship of men from sinking back in the 1940s. During the winter months when my dad was not fishing for cod, he was back in Figueira da Foz, fishing for sardines on the "Traineiras".

Fried Salted Cod with Sautéed Onions / Bacalhau Frito com Cebolada

Makes 4 servings

4 pieces salted cod, desalted
1½ cups olive oil
Flour to coat fish
3 medium onions, cut into thin half moon slices

1 bay leaf
3 garlic cloves, minced
Chopped parsley to garnish

....

Desalt cod ahead of time by soaking in a large bowl of cold water, making sure to cover completely, for at least 24 hours and up to 48 hours (depending on the thickness of the cod). Refrigerate and change water approximately every six hours. The first change of water should be about two hours after initial soaking.

Heat olive oil in a large frying pan.

Put enough flour to coat fish in a wide shallow dish. Pat cod pieces dry with a paper towel and dredge them in flour one piece at a time.

Add floured cod pieces into the pan. Fry on both sides until cod turns a golden, toasty color. Remove fried cod from frying pan and place on a plate lined with a paper towel to soak up some of the oil.

In the same frying pan, add onions, bay leaf and garlic. Fry until onions become translucent and slightly browned. (NOTE: you may use the same oil to fry onions that was used to fry cod if it is still clean. Otherwise, allow the used oil to cool, dispose of it and add a new cup of olive oil to fry onions or simply use another frying pan).

Transfer cod to a serving tray. Pour fried onions and garlic over fried cod. Garnish with fresh chopped parsley. This dish is typically served with round, hand cut fries as a side.

Salted Cod Gomes de Sá Style / Bacalhau à Gomes de Sá

Makes 6 to 8 servings

5 pieces salted cod
6 medium potatoes
4 medium onions, sliced crosswise
2 garlic cloves, minced
3 hard boiled eggs, peeled and sliced crosswise

1½ cups olive oil, divided
2 tablespoons chopped parsley
Black olives
Salt and pepper to taste

....

Desalt cod ahead of time by soaking in a large bowl of cold water, making sure to cover completely, for at least 24 hours and up to 48 hours (depending on the thickness of the cod). Refrigerate and change water approximately every six hours. The first change of water should be about two hours after initial soaking.

After desalted, boil cod for approximately 10 minutes. Remove from water and allow to cool. In the same water cod was boiled in, cook potatoes with skins on. Boil potatoes until tender, but not overcooked (approximately 30 minutes). Remove potatoes from water and set aside to cool.

In a separate pan, boil eggs for approximately 12 minutes. Place boiled eggs in cold water immediately and remove eggshells. Cut eggs into thin round slices after cooled. Set aside.

After cod has cooled, remove skin, debone and flake. After potatoes have cooled remove skin and cut into ⅓ inch oval slices or ¾ inch cubes.

In a frying pan, sauté onions and garlic in ½ cup of olive oil. Once onions start to become translucent and turning golden, remove from heat.

Preheat the oven to 350 degrees F. In a baking or casserole dish, add potatoes and cod. Pour sautéed onions, garlic and olive oil from the frying pan over it. Drizzle generously with the rest of olive oil and sprinkle pepper onto the mixture. If you find that cod is not salty enough after being desalted, add a little salt. Gently mix all ingredients.

Place in the oven at 350 degrees F for approximately 30 minutes or until potatoes start to turn a golden color. Once cooked, remove baking dish from the oven. Garnish with chopped parsley, black olives and sliced hard-boiled eggs.

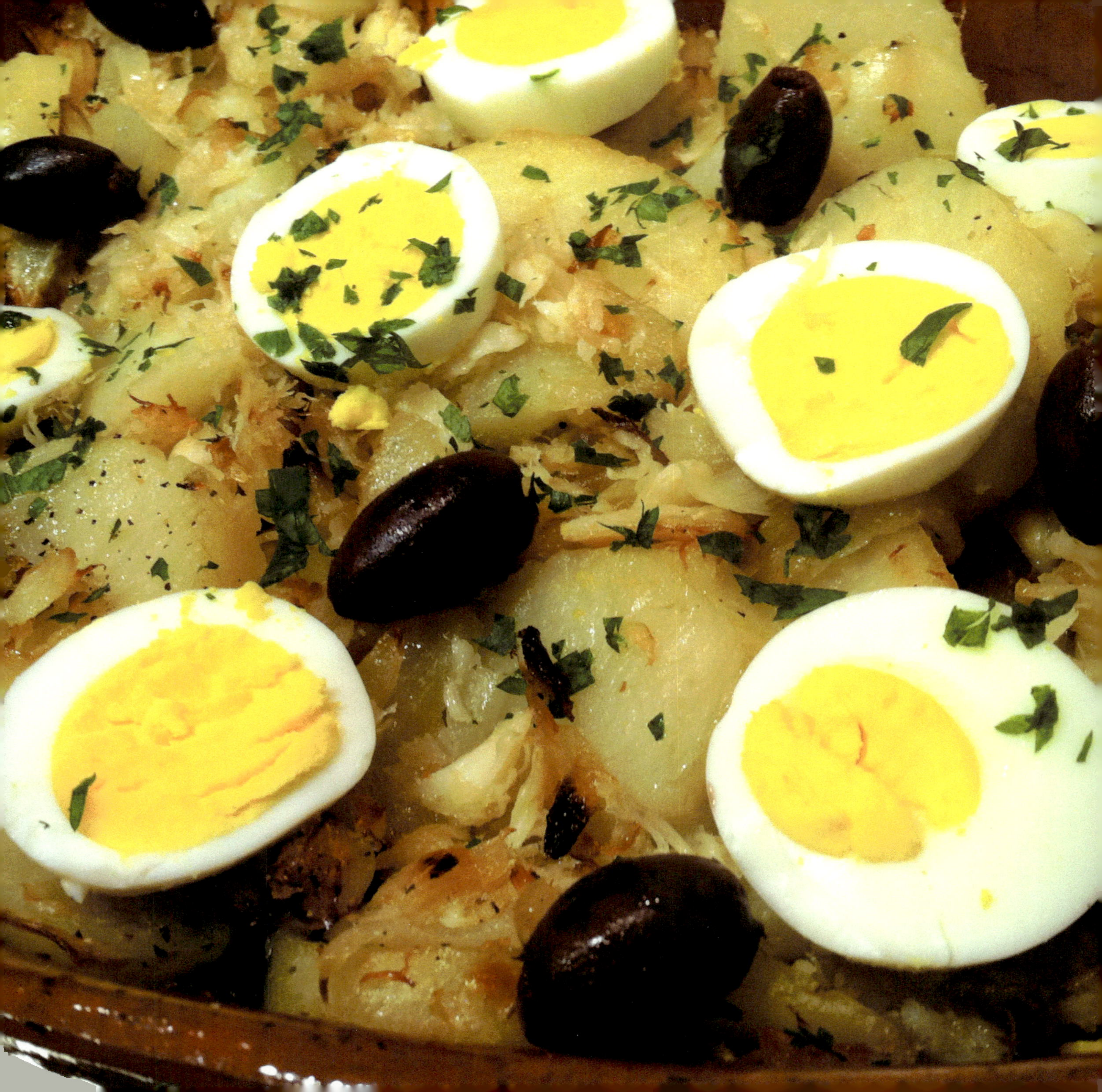

Salted Cod with Eggs and Fries / Bacalhau à Brás

Makes 4 to 6 servings

4 pieces salted cod
8 potatoes, peeled and cut into matchstick thin slices
Vegetable or canola oil to fry potatoes
½ cup olive oil
3 medium onions, cut into thin half moon slices

3 garlic cloves, minced
8 eggs
Salt and pepper to taste
3 tablespoons parsley, chopped
Black olives to garnish

....

Desalt cod ahead of time by soaking in a large bowl of cold water, making sure to cover completely, for at least 24 hours and up to 48 hours (depending on the thickness of the cod). Refrigerate and change water approximately every six hours. The first change of water should be about two hours after initial soaking.

Boil desalted cod for approximately 10 minutes. Set aside to cool. Once cod has cooled, debone and flake into small pieces.

Peel and cut potatoes into thin, matchstick length sizes. Fry potatoes in vegetable or canola oil until golden and crispy. Place fries on a plate lined with a paper towel to soak up oil and set aside.

Heat olive oil in a large skillet. Add onion and garlic. Sauté until onions become translucent.

Add flaked cod to sautéed onions and garlic. Toss cod around so that it is well coated with olive oil and onions.

In the meantime, crack eggs in a bowl, season with salt and pepper and whisk well.

Next, add fries to cod and onions in the skillet. Allow to brown a bit and then slowly pour the eggs on top, gently mixing as you do so.

When eggs are just about cooked, add parsley and toss well. When eggs are fully cooked, remove Bacalhau à Brás from skillet and place on a tray. Top with olives and serve. Garnish with some additional chopped parsley (optional).

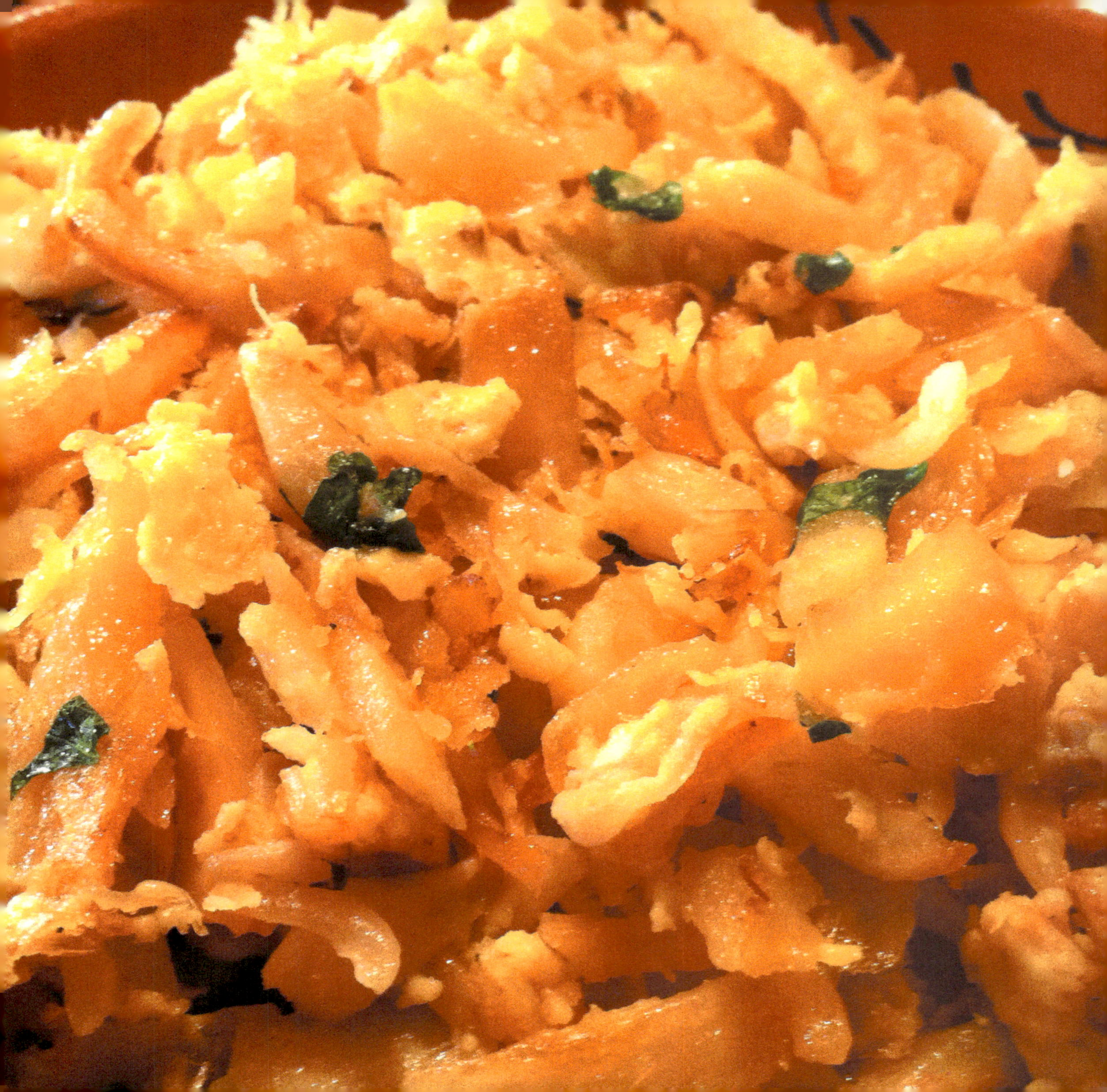

Salted Cod Lagareiro Style / Bacalhau à Lagareiro

Makes 4 servings

4 pieces salted cod
2 cups olive oil
5 garlic cloves, minced
10 to 12 small or medium gold potatoes

Sea salt to taste
2 medium onions, sliced thin and crosswise
1 sprig parsley, chopped

....

Desalt cod ahead of time by soaking cod in a large bowl of cold water, making sure to cover completely, for at least 24 hours and up to 48 hours (depending on thickness of cod). Refrigerate and change water approximately every six hours. The first change of water should be about two hours after initial soaking.

Preheat the oven to 400 degrees F. Place desalted cod in a baking dish. Pour olive oil and garlic over cod.

Wash potatoes well, leaving the skin on. Dry potatoes off with a paper towel and poke a few holes in potatoes with a fork or make a small slice in each with a knife. In a separate shallow metal tray, lay a bed of sea salt. Place potatoes on top of salt and sprinkle a little of this sea salt over potatoes.

Place the baking dish with cod and the metal tray with potatoes in a preheated oven. As cod is baking, occasionally drizzle with olive oil already in the baking dish. When cod is almost baked, place sliced onions in the baking dish with cod (approximately 15 minutes before removing cod from oven).

Bake potatoes and cod for approximately 50 minutes or until potatoes and cod become a golden, toasty color. When potatoes are done, remove from oven. While potatoes are still warm, but not too hot to handle, shake off any sea salt stuck to potatoes or use a paper towel to hold them and rub off most of salt. On a flat surface, place dishcloth over each potato and then punch it.

Place punched potatoes on a serving tray / dish and then cod on top. Pour olive oil with garlic from the baking dish over cod and potatoes. Place sliced onions on top of cod. Garnish with fresh chopped parsley and serve.

Salted Cod with Heavy Cream / Bacalhau com Natas

Makes 6 to 8 servings

5 or 6 pieces salted cod
3 pounds potatoes, peeled and cut into cubes
Vegetable / canola oil to fry potatoes
½ cup olive oil

2 large onions, sliced thin crosswise
1 bay leaf
3 garlic cloves, minced

Bechamel sauce:
2 tablespoons unsalted butter
2 tablespoons flour
1 cup milk

1 pint heavy cream
½ teaspoon ground nutmeg (optional)
Salt and pepper to taste

....

Desalt cod ahead of time by soaking cod in a large bowl of cold water, making sure to cover completely, for at least 24 hours and up to 48 hours (depending on thickness of cod). Refrigerate and change water approximately every six hours. The first change of water should be about two hours after initial soaking.

Boil cod for approximately 10 minutes, drain and set aside to cool. Once cooled, flake cod into small pieces removing all bones and skin.

Heat vegetable / canola oil in large frying pan. Add potatoes and fry until cooked through and turning golden.

In a separate frying pan, heat olive oil. Add onions, bay leaf and garlic. Fry until onions become translucent and start to brown a little. Add cod and fried potatoes to the frying pan and mix well.

Preheat oven to 350 degrees F.

Bechamel sauce:
Melt butter in a saucepan. Slowly add flour and mix well. Next, add milk, heavy cream, and mix well again. Add nutmeg, salt and pepper and cook over low heat until sauce starts to thicken and becomes creamy.

Place cod / potatoes mixture in a large oven safe baking dish and pour Bechamel sauce on top. Bake for approximately 20 minutes. Turn up the heat for an additional few minutes until golden brown.

Stewed Squid with Potatoes / Lulas Guisadas com Batatas

Makes 4 servings

1¼ pounds fresh squid tubes and tentacles
⅓ cup olive oil
2 medium onions, chopped
2 garlic cloves, minced
1 bay leaf
2 ripe tomatoes, peeled, seeded and cubed
2 teaspoons tomato paste

3 parsley sprigs, chopped
½ cup white wine
1 cup water, divided
Salt and pepper to taste
8 medium potatoes, peeled and cubed
Dash of hot sauce (optional)

....

Clean squid by rinsing it well and removing tentacles and cartilage found in tube part of body. This cartilage is not edible. However, tentacles are edible and can be used in the stew (optional). Cut squid tubes into rings or rectangular shapes. Keep in mind that squid shrinks, so do not cut the pieces too small.

Heat olive oil in a saucepan. Add onions, garlic and bay leaf and sauté until onions become translucent.

Add tomatoes, tomato paste and parsley. Allow to simmer for approximately 10 minutes.

Add squid and simmer on medium heat for a few minutes.

Add wine, ½ cup of water and bring to a boil. Season with salt and pepper to taste. Reduce heat, cover and allow to simmer on low.

After approximately 30 minutes, add the other ½ cup of water, bring to a boil and add potatoes. If you like this dish a little spicy, add a dash of hot sauce. Allow to cook for another 20 minutes or until potatoes are cooked. Garnish with additional fresh chopped parsley.

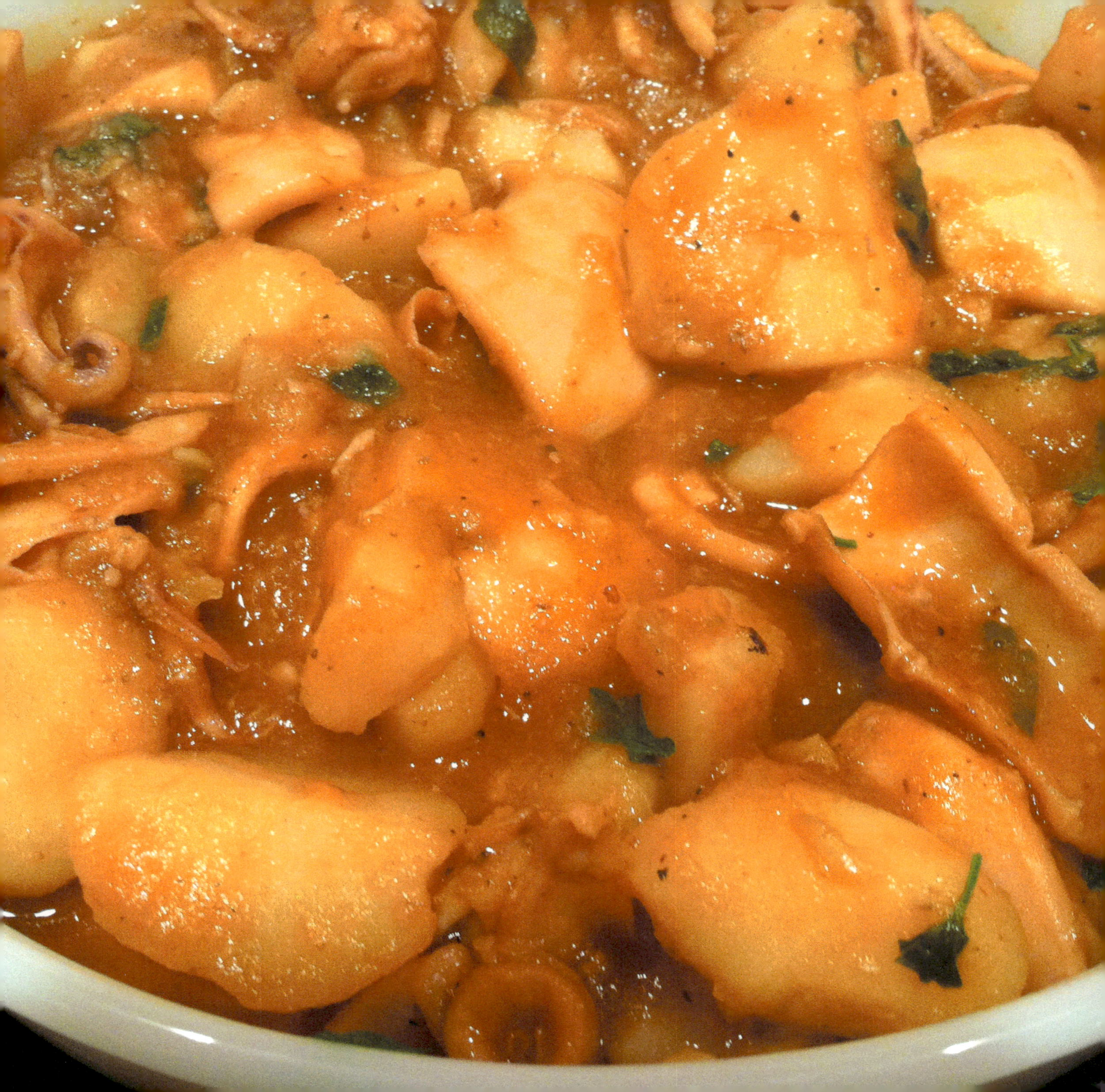

Stewed Squid with Rice / Lulas Guisadas com Arroz

Makes 4 servings

1¼ pounds fresh squid tubes and tentacles
⅓ cup olive oil
2 medium onions, chopped
2 garlic cloves, minced
1 bay leaf
2 ripe tomatoes, peeled and cubed
2 teaspoons tomato paste

3 parsley sprigs, chopped
½ cup white wine
1 cup water, divided
Salt and pepper to taste
1 cup rice
Dash of hot sauce (optional)

....

Clean squid by rinsing it well and removing tentacles and cartilage found in tube part of body. This cartilage is not edible. However, tentacles are edible and can be used in the stew (optional). Cut squid tubes into rings or rectangular shapes. Keep in mind that squid shrinks, so do not cut the pieces too small.

Heat olive oil in a saucepan. Add onions, garlic and bay leaf and sauté until the onions become translucent.

Add tomatoes, tomato paste and parsley. Allow to simmer for approximately 10 minutes.

Add squid and simmer on medium heat for a few minutes.

Add wine, ½ cup of water and bring to a boil. Reduce heat, cover and allow to simmer on low. Season with salt and pepper to taste. If desired, add a dash of hot sauce.

After 30 minutes, add the other ½ cup of water, bring to a boil and then add rice. Allow to cook for another 15 minutes or until rice is cooked. If rice starts to become dry, add a little more water. This dish should not be allowed to dry out. It is meant to be served soupy (referred to as "malandro" in Portuguese).

Baked Fish with Potatoes / Peixe Assado com Batatas

Makes 4 servings

1 whole fish, scaled and gutted (such as flounder, yellowtail, hake or sea bass)
Salt and pepper to taste
6 potatoes, peeled and sliced into quarters, wedged or cubed
2 garlic cloves, minced
2 tablespoons ollve oil
1 heaping teaspoon tomato paste

1 medium onion, cut into round slices
1 bay leaf
2 tomatoes, peeled and cubed
1 cup white wine
Olive oil (to drizzle over fish and potatoes)
1 tablespoon fresh parsley, chopped
Water as needed

---

30 minutes ahead of time, season fish with salt and pepper. Cut two diagonal slices on one side of fish and keep this side facing up.

Boil potatoes in water seasoned with salt for approximately 20 minutes to accelerate baking time of potatoes and then drain. Set potatoes aside until ready to bake fish.

Mix minced garlic, olive oil and tomato paste in a small bowl. Spread some of this mixture onto fish on both sides and put remainder in the middle of the baking dish. Place sliced onions and bay leaf on top of tomato paste mixture. Place fish on top of onions. Add tomatoes and potatoes around fish. Pour wine and drizzle some olive oil over fish and potatoes. Top with chopped parsley.

Bake at 350 degrees F for approximately 45 minutes to 1 hour, depending on size and thickness of fish. When fish looks like it is getting a little browned, increase temperature to 400 / 425 degrees F in order to brown potatoes. Remove from oven when potatoes start to become golden and a little toasty.

Note: While fish and potatoes are baking, add a little water as needed so that the baking dish does not dry out completely and so that there is a little sauce left to drizzle over potatoes.

Monk fish Stew / Caldeirada de Tamboril

Makes 4 to 6 servings

3 to 4 pounds monkfish
4 onions, peeled and sliced thin crosswise
4 garlic cloves, peeled and sliced crosswise
2 bay leaves
1 green bell pepper, cut into thin small strips
1 red bell pepper, cut into thin small strips
3 ripe tomatoes, peeled, seeded and cubed
8 medium potatoes, peeled and cut into oval slices ½" thick

Olive oil
1 teaspoon paprika
1 cup beer or white wine
3 to 4 cups water or fish broth
1 sprig parsley
Salt and pepper to taste
4 tablespoons tomato paste
Dash of hot sauce (optional)

....

Prepare fish by removing skin, center cartilage and spiny fins on the sides. Cut into 1 - 1 ½" square medallions. Season with salt and pepper and set aside for at least an hour. You may skip this step if you purchase the monkfish already with the cartilage and spiny fins removed.

If you have purchased the entire monkfish, you can create your own fish broth by boiling monkfish cartilage that you removed in a large pot. Use this broth instead of water for an even more flavorful fish stew.

Place ingredients in layers starting with onion on the bottom. On top of onion slices, add garlic, bay leaves, peppers, tomatoes and last, add layer of potatoes. Drizzle some olive oil and sprinkle paprika over ingredients. Next, add wine (or beer) and water or (fish stock) and parsley sprig. Also, add a little salt and pepper. Cover and bring to a boil.

Reduce the heat to medium and add tomato paste, blending well. You may also add a dash of hot sauce if you choose. Cook for approximately 20 minutes and then add fish as the top layer. Bring to a boil covered. Allow to cook covered for a few minutes and then remove cover and allow to cook until the fish is completely cooked and the sauce has thickened a bit. Test sauce for flavor and if it needs more salt, add some at this time while you are allowing the sauce to thicken.

NOTE: Other fish such as hake, haddock, cod or redfish can be used in place of the monkfish. If you use one of these other kinds of fish, it is traditionally cut into about 1- 1" slices with skin on (scales removed) and bones in.

Small Fried Sardines with Escabeche Sauce / Petinga Frita com Molho Escabeche

Makes 4 to 6 servings

2 pounds small sardines, gutted
Course sea salt to taste
Flour to coat
Vegetable or canola oil for frying

....

Season sardines with salt. Allow to sit 15 - 30 minutes.

In a large frying pan, add enough oil to fry fish (approximately ½ inch up the sides of pan). Heat oil over high – medium until hot. Coat each sardine with flour and add to hot oil. Fry on both sides until sardines start to turn golden and crispy. Remove sardines and place on a flat dish lined with a paper towel to absorb excess oil.

Eat as is or topped with Escabeche Sauce (recipe below). These taste great with tomato rice as a side.

For Escabeche Sauce:
½ cup olive oil
2 onions, sliced thin into half moon slices
5 garlic cloves, minced
2 bay leaves
1 teaspoon of paprika
White vinegar to taste
Salt and pepper to taste

....

Heat olive oil in a large frying pan. Add onions, garlic and bay leaves. Sauté for about 1 to 2 minutes, being careful not to burn garlic. Add paprika, vinegar, salt and pepper to taste and bring to a boil. Reduce heat and cover until onions are translucent, stirring occasionally with a wooden spoon. Pour over fried fish that has been cooled.

Seafood Macaroni / Massada de Marisco

Makes 8 to 10 servings

1 pound monkfish
Salt and pepper to taste
1 pound fresh littleneck clams
1 pound shrimp (fresh or frozen)
2 medium onions, chopped
2 garlic cloves, minced
1 bay leaf
½ cup olive oil
2 tablespoons tomato paste

1 cup wine
1 cup water
2 ripe tomatoes, peeled and cubed
½ green pepper sliced into thin long slices
Dash hot sauce
2 tablespoons chopped parsley
1 box (16 ounces) macaroni
2 parsley sprigs to garnish

....

Cut monkfish into small pieces, approximately one inch thick. Season with salt and pepper about 1 hour ahead of time.

Soak clams in water and scrub them to clean any particles or grit from the outside surface. Lift clams out of water into another bowl of clean water. Do not simply dump clams into the second bowl, as you will also dump sand along with clams. Do this a couple of times to ensure that the sand has been removed. Note: Fresh clams may be soaked in water with salt overnight to encourage them to squirt some of the sand out.

In a medium pot, cook shrimp and clams in water seasoned with salt to taste.

In a separate large pot, sauté onions, garlic and bay leaf in olive oil. When onions become translucent, add tomato paste, wine, water and bring to a boil. Add tomatoes, green pepper, hot sauce, parsley and salt. Bring to a boil again and then reduce heat to a simmer until tomatoes are almost cooked.

When tomatoes start to become soft, add more water along with broth from shrimp and clam pot, making sure enough is added to cook macaroni (per package). Bring to a boil once again. Add entire box of macaroni. Allow macaroni to cook approximately 5 minutes and then add monkfish. Also, add cooked shrimp and clams (only those with shells open). If needed, add more broth from the pot used to cook clams and shrimp. Be sure to add enough broth to allow for a very wet seafood macaroni. This dish should be served immediately while pasta is soupy. Use additional parsley to garnish.

Note: Do not allow broth to dry up at any time during cooking process. If it does, simply add more water from the pot where shrimp and clams were cooked. You may also add scallops to this dish or use mussels instead of clams. It is a matter of personal preference.

GiFT + CRAFT
GOURMET

Mercearia
& Ideias

Meat and Chicken / Carne e Galinha

- Simple Portuguese Steak / Prego no Prato
- Portuguese Steak with Sauce / Bife à Casa
- Pot Roast / Carne Assada
- Beef with Onions / Bife de Cebolada
- Pork Ribs / Entrecosto
- Pork Sandwiches / Bifanas
- Stewed Pork Chops with Potatoes / Caldeirada de Costeletas
- Roasted Pork Loin / Lombo de Porco Assado
- Piri Piri Chicken / Frango Assado com Piri Piri
- Chicken Stew / Galinha Guisada
- Chicken Stew with Peas and Potatoes / Galinha à Jardineira
- Boiled Dinner / Cozido à Portuguesa

The Portuguese steak is a favorite of many fans of Portuguese food. The Portuguese Steak can be prepared with a sauce or without a sauce. I like it both ways, but few things taste better than a good steak with a savory sauce. The first recipe below is what I like to call the Simple Steak, which has no sauce. This steak is typically a very thin steak just fried in oil with some garlic and bay leaves. In Portugal, this is often called Prego no Prato, which translated literally, means Nail on the Plate. Leave it to the Portuguese to come up with some creative names for their delicious food!

Simple Portuguese Steak / Prego no Prato

Makes 6 servings

6 thin sirloin steaks
Salt and pepper to taste
6 garlic cloves, smashed

3 bay leaves
2 garlic cloves, sliced crosswise
½ cup olive or canola / vegetable oil

Pound steaks with meat tenderizer on both sides. Season steaks with salt and pepper to taste and spread mashed garlic over each. Add half a bay leaf to each steak as well. Allow to sit for 1-2 hours.

In a large frying pan, heat oil, add sliced garlic cloves and then seasoned steaks along with smashed garlic and bay leaves. Fry steaks on both sides to your liking. (You may need to fry steaks in two batches). When steaks are done, place on a serving dish and pour oil / fried garlic over steaks.

Serve with homemade french fries, white rice and a sunny side up egg on top of steak.

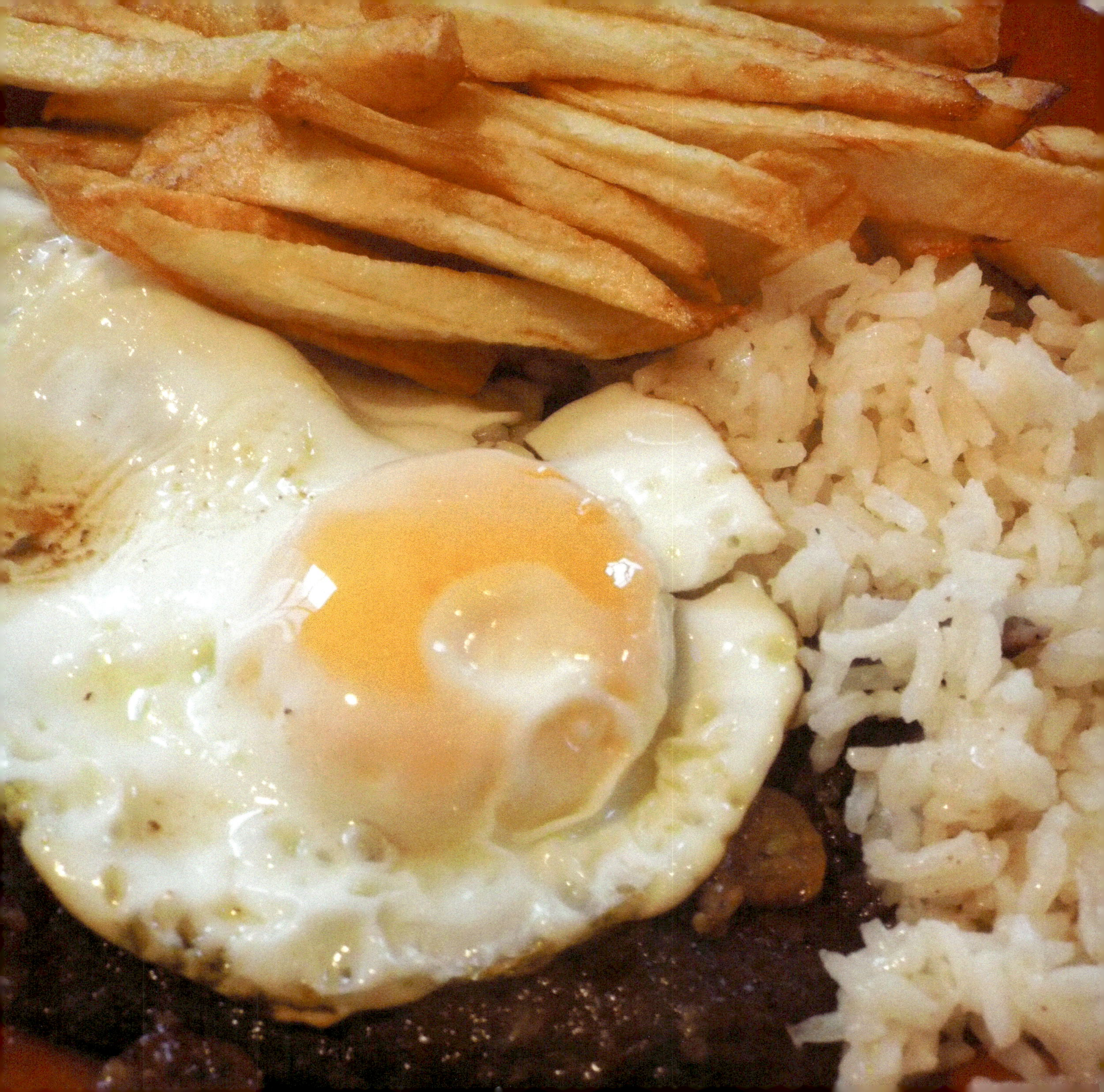

Portuguese Steak with Sauce / Bife à Casa

Makes 4 servings

4 sirloin steaks about 8 ounces each and ½" thick
Coarse sea salt and pepper to taste
⅓ cup olive oil
6 garlic cloves, smashed
2 bay leaves, cut in half
½ cup white wine

2 tablespoons butter
1 tablespoon red wine vinegar
3 tablespoons milk / heavy cream
1 teaspoon hot crushed pepper sauce
 ("pimenta moida")

....

Remove steaks from refrigerator and allow to reach room temperature. A few minutes before ready to fry steaks, season with coarse sea salt and pepper on both sides.

In a large frying pan, heat olive oil and then add garlic and bay leaves. Add the steaks and fry for 2 to 3 minutes on each side. Remove steaks from pan. To frying pan, add wine, butter and red wine vinegar. Allow to reduce slightly. Add milk / heavy cream and hot crushed pepper sauce. Allow to reduce some more until the sauce thickens a bit.

Return steak to the pan along with any juices released from steaks and cook to your liking.

Place each individual steak on a plate and pour some sauce over each. Serve with homemade, hand cut french fries, rice and a fried sunny side up egg on top. A slice of grilled ham can also be added between egg and steak.

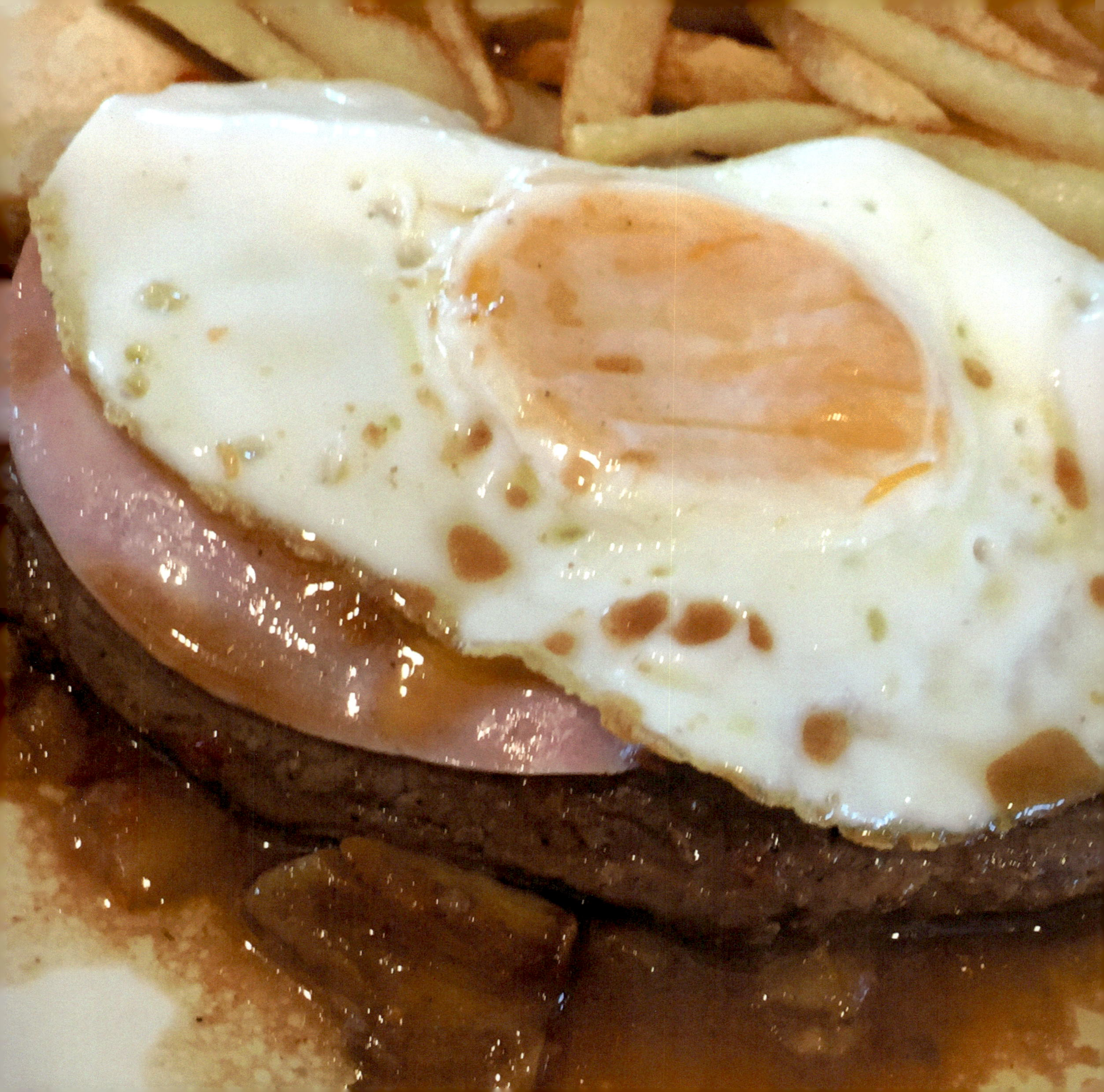

Pot Roast / Carne Assada

Makes 6 to 8 servings

4 to 5 pound bottom round roast
1 onion, sliced thin crosswise
1 cup beer
Coarse sea salt and pepper to taste
1 teaspoon paprika

2 cloves garlic, minced
2 bay leaves
Olive oil
1 cup water

....

Place roast, with fat side facing up, on top of onion slices in the center of a Pyrex dish. Pour beer over roast.

Rub roast with sea salt all over and sprinkle with pepper and paprika. Spread minced garlic over roast. Place one bay leaf cut in half on top of roast and second bay leaf underneath roast. Drizzle with olive oil. Allow roast to sit for about an hour.

Preheat oven to 400 degrees F. Add water directly into Pyrex dish (do not pour over roast) and place roast in the oven. Roast meat for approximately 30 minutes and then reduce oven temperature to 300 degrees F. Let roast cook at 300 degrees F for 2 to 3 hours. If at any time juices in the Pyrex start to dry up, add a little more water.

During last 30 minutes or so, increase temperature to 350 degrees F until juices start flowing from meat and onions are translucent. Remove from oven when meat is cooked to your liking and allow to sit for 15 minutes before carving.

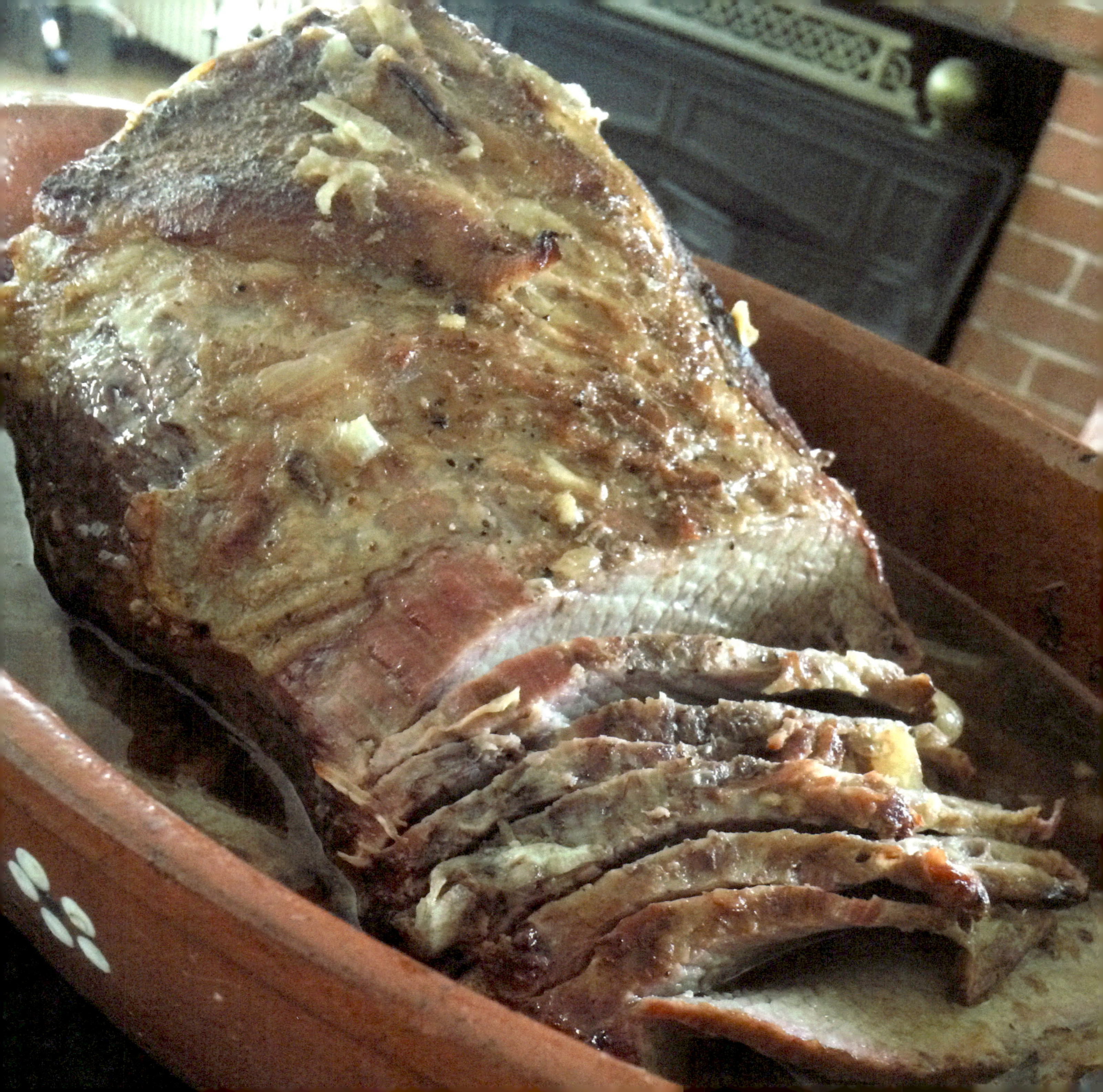

My mother did not make meat dishes too often, but this is one that was a regular in her house. The tomato / onion sauce in this dish tastes just perfect with a side of mashed potatoes.

Beef with Onions / Bife de Cebolada

Makes 4 servings

1¼ pounds thin slices of sirloin or rump beef
Salt and pepper to taste
⅓ cup olive oil
3 onions, sliced thin and crosswise
2 garlic cloves, minced
1 bay leaf

1 sprig parsley, chopped
2 ripe tomatoes, peeled and cubed
1 tablespoon of tomato paste
1 cup white wine
2½ cups water, divided

....

Approximately one hour ahead of time, season beef slices with salt and pepper to taste.

In a medium pot, heat olive oil and then add onions, garlic, bay leaf and parsley.

When onions start to become translucent, add tomatoes, tomato paste, wine, salt, pepper and one cup of water. Bring to a boil. Reduce heat and allow to simmer for approximately 10 minutes or until tomatoes soften.

Add beef and remaining amount of water (1.5 cups) or enough to just cover beef. Bring to a boil, reduce to low heat and cook covered for approximately 30 minutes or until beef is cooked. If sauce remains too watery, remove cover from pan, and cook for a few additional minutes in order to thicken sauce.

Serve with mashed potatoes or other side dish of choice.

When it comes to ribs, the simpler the better in my opinion. I like to taste the flavor of the meat, and this recipe allows for just that. "Entrecosto" is very popular in Portugal and is prepared with very simple ingredients. We make these often in the summer. I season them, and my husband grills them to perfection. My mother always tells us these are the best ribs she's ever had!!

Pork Ribs / Entrecosto

Makes 4 to 6 servings

1 rack pork ribs
Sea salt and pepper to taste
2 teaspoons paprika
1 tablespoon olive oil

Hot sauce or hot crushed pepper sauce ("pimenta moida") to taste
1 bay leaf, cut in half

Rub rack of ribs with sea salt. Sprinkle with black pepper and paprika.

Drizzle with olive oil and a little hot sauce / hot crushed pepper sauce. Place bay leaf halves on ribs and let marinate for 1 to 2 hours.

Place ribs on heated outdoor gas or charcoal grill. Grill ribs until tender and browned. When done, slice between the ribs, place on a tray and serve.

Note: You may also squeeze a little lemon juice onto the ribs when marinating.

One of the tastiest meat sandwiches, in my opinion, is the Bifana: deliciously seasoned thin slices of pork loin in a fresh Portuguese roll (Papo Seco). I love a good Bifana with a little mustard, a strip of Malagueta (red hot pepper) on top and a side of homemade fries, of course.

Pork Sandwiches / Bifanas

Makes 8 to 10 servings

2 pounds pork loin, cut into thin slices
5 garlic cloves, minced
Salt, pepper and paprika to taste
Hot crushed pepper sauce
    ("pimenta moida")

3 bay leaves, cut in half
1 cup white wine
Lemon juice from ½ - 1 lemon
Olive oil

....

Pound cutlets to tenderize. In a Pyrex or large flat baking dish, layer pork cutlets and season them with garlic, salt, pepper, paprika, hot crushed pepper sauce and bay leaves, making sure to cover all of the cutlets. Pour lemon juice and wine over pork and allow to marinate for a few hours or overnight in the refrigerator. When you are ready to fry pork cutlets, remove from the refrigerator and allow to reach room temperature before frying.

In a large frying pan, heat olive oil (or lard if you so choose). Remove pork cutlets from marinade, dry them a bit in a paper towel to remove some of the excess wetness and add to hot frying pan.

Fry cutlets at medium to high heat and flip the them so they cook on both sides. When cutlets start to brown, remove from frying pan. While the last batch of cutlets are frying, add the remaining wine marinade to frying pan and cook until they are done. At the end, return all cutlets back to the frying pan so that they are coated with the marinade remaining in the pan.

When ready to serve, place the pork cutlets in fresh Papo Secos (Portuguese Bread Rolls). May be served with a thin slice of hot red pepper and mustard may be added to the sandwich. Typically, hand-cut homemade french fries are served as a side with Bifanas.

Note: Traditionally lard is used to fry the cutlets, but olive oil is another option.

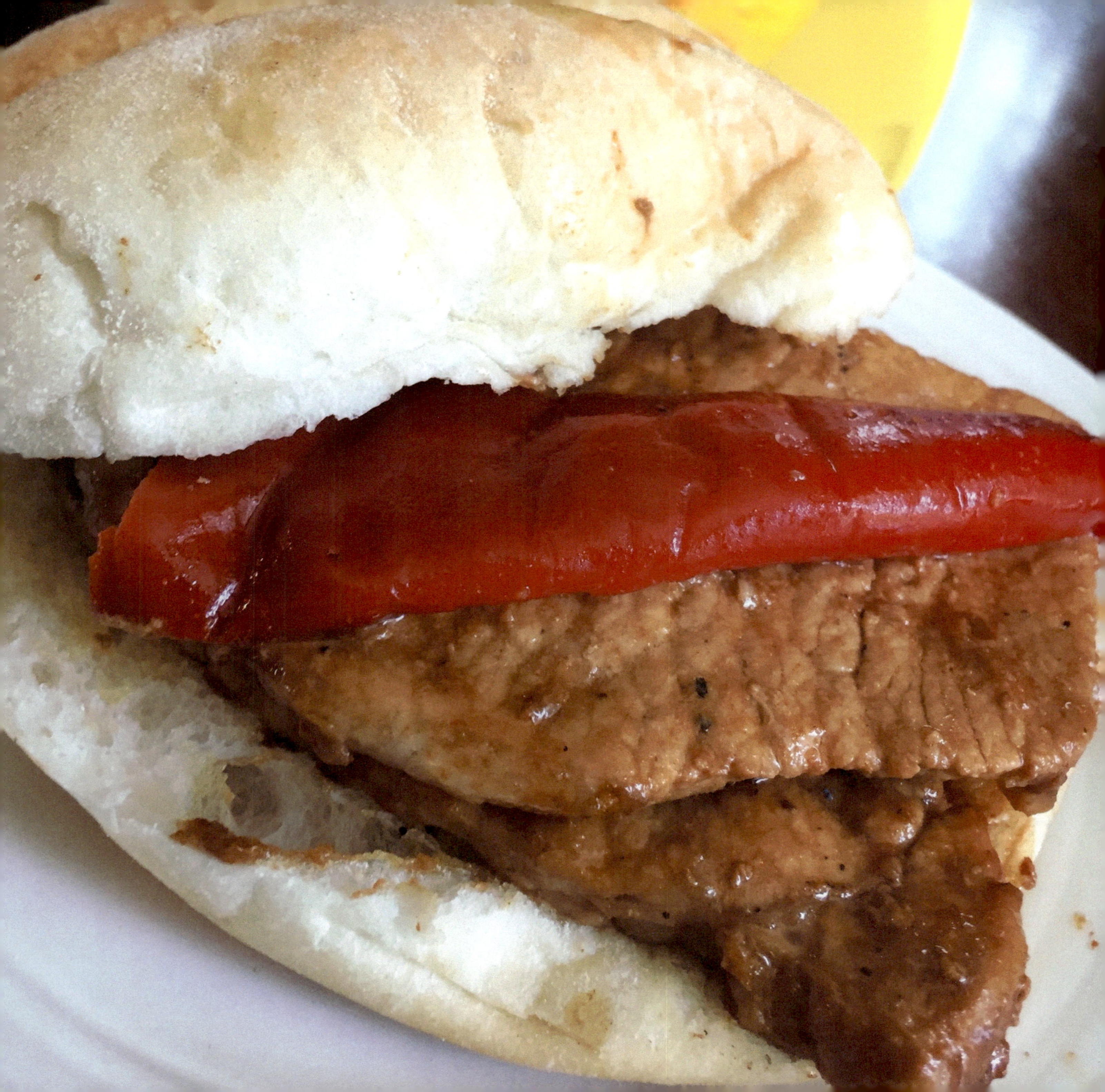

Typically when you hear the word "caldeirada" you think of fish stew, but you can also make a caldeirada with pork chops. This is a delicious dish and a great alternative to frying or baking pork chops. For me, this dish tastes best when drizzled with some vinegar over it.

Stewed Pork Chops with Potatoes / Caldeirada de Costeletas

Makes 4 servings

4 pork chops
Salt, pepper and garlic powder to taste
5 medium potatoes
2 medium onions, sliced thin crosswise
1 tablespoon olive oil
2 garlic cloves, minced

2 ripe tomatoes, peeled and cubed
3 tablespoons tomato paste
8 small thin slices red pepper
1 bay leaf
1 cup beer or white wine
Water, enough to cover

Season pork chops with salt, pepper and garlic powder about an hour before.

Peel potatoes and cut them crosswise into slices about ½" thick.

In a medium pot, place sliced onions at the bottom. Place potatoes on top of onions. Drizzle olive oil on top of potatoes. Next, add garlic, tomatoes, tomato paste, red pepper, bay leaf, beer / wine and enough water to cover potatoes. Also, add more salt and pepper to taste.

Bring everything to a boil. Reduce heat and simmer at low medium heat. Cook all ingredients for 20 minutes or so, and then add pork chops. Continue to simmer at low medium heat with cover on until pork chops are cooked, onions are translucent and sauce starts to thicken a little. Before turning off the stove, simmer on low without the cover for a few minutes to allow sauce to thicken a little more. The sauce should not be too watery. For added flavor, drizzle with vinegar once served on your plate.

Roasted Pork Loin / Lombo de Porco Assado

Makes 6 to 8 servings

3 to 4 pounds boneless pork loin
½ cup white wine
⅓ cup olive oil
4 garlic cloves, smashed / crushed
1 teaspoon coarse sea salt or to taste
½ teaspoon ground black pepper or to taste

1½ teaspoons hot crushed pepper sauce ("pimenta moida")
1 tablespoon paprika
2 bay leaves
Water as required

....

Pork loin may be marinated up to 24 hours ahead of time for additional flavor. This is not necessary, but try to marinate for at least an hour or two before roasting.

To marinate, pour wine over meat after poking a few holes in meat with a fork or knife. Drizzle olive oil on both sides of roast. In a small bowl, combine garlic, salt, pepper, hot crushed pepper sauce and paprika. Rub roast with this mixture and add bay leaves. Cover and refrigerate if marinating for a long period of time.

When ready to make roast, remove pork loin from the refrigerator and allow to reach room temperature. Preheat oven to 450 degrees F. Place pork loin in a roasting pan with fat side facing up, cover with foil and place in oven. After 15 minutes reduce heat to 300 degrees F. Allow to cook for approximately 1 hour. After that, remove the foil and increase to 350 degrees F to brown slightly. At any point, if juices in the pan start to dry up, add a little water. Remove when roast is cooked. Allow to cool for approximately 15 minutes before slicing and serving.

May be served with the juices as is in the roasting pan or a thicker gravy can be made separately. Simply remove any juices / drippings in the roasting pan and place in a saucepan heating it on the stovetop. In a small bowl, add 2 teaspoons of flour to a bit of water and whisk it well until all lumps are removed. Add this mixture to the saucepan and blend well. Allow to simmer so that gravy reduces and thickens. Pour gravy over pork loin when serving.

Note: Peeled carrots may also be added to this dish and baked along with pork loin.

Piri Piri Chicken / Frango Assado com Piri Piri

Makes 4 servings

1 small whole chicken (between 3 - 4 pounds)
1 to 1½ tablespoons coarse sea salt
1 to 2 tablespoons Piri Piri sauce or hot sauce
2 tablespoons olive oil

Juice of one lemon
Pepper to taste
4 garlic cloves, smashed

....

Make a vertical cut down the middle of the breast of chicken. Turn chicken over and using palm of your hand flatten it out. Remove any excess fat.

Rub salt on both sides of chicken. In a small bowl, combine piri-piri / hot sauce, olive oil, lemon juice, pepper and garlic. Blend well. Baste chicken on both sides with mixture and make cuts near wings and drumsticks. Allow to marinate for at least two hours.

Preheat oven to 400 degrees F. Place chicken on a rack on top of a shallow roasting pan. Add three cups of water in the pan. (This keeps chicken from making a mess of your oven, and you can also use the drippings as gravy if you like).

Place chicken in the oven and allow to cook for a little over an hour or until chicken is fully cooked. Also, turn chicken a couple of times to get it toasty on both sides. As chicken is roasting, you may baste some additional piri piri sauce or drippings from the pan on it.

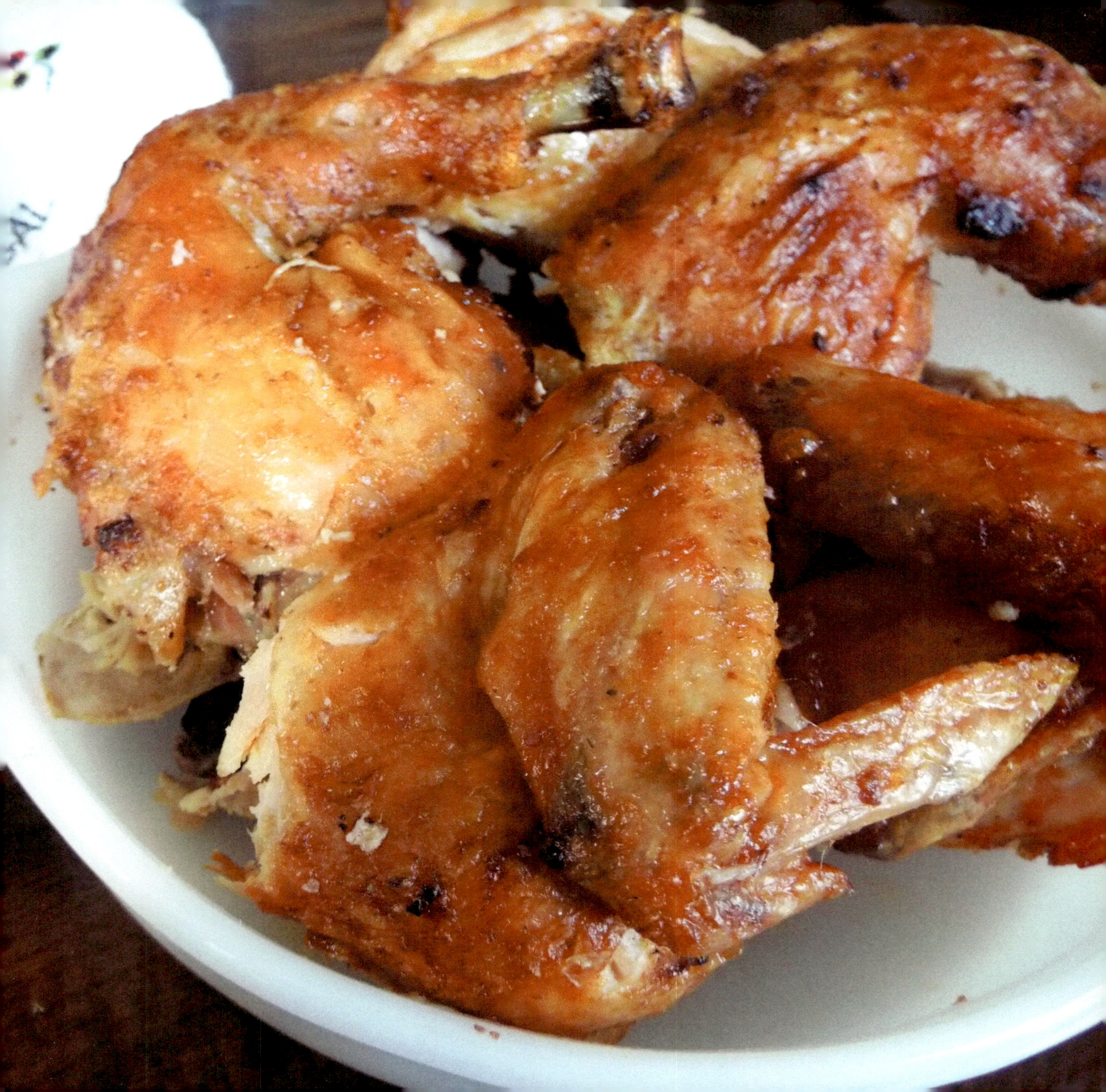

Growing up, stews were popular in our house, and Chicken Stew was a regular. Sometimes, my mom added spaghetti to this dish. Other times, she would simply make the chicken and serve mashed potatoes on the side. Either way she served her Chicken Stew, it was delicious!

Chicken Stew / Galinha Guisada

Makes 6 to 8 servings

6 to 8 pieces of chicken legs or thighs
1 cup white wine or beer
Salt and pepper to taste
3 garlic cloves, minced and divided
½ cup olive oil
1 onion, minced
1 bay leaf

1 tablespoon tomato paste
2 tomatoes, peeled and cubed
2 - 3 carrots, peeled and cut into thin round slices
1 tablespoon parsley, coarsely chopped
1 cup water
1 box spaghetti (optional)

....

Remove most or all skin and excess fat from chicken. Pour wine / beer over chicken. Season chicken with salt, pepper and half of minced garlic, approximately 4 hours ahead of time.

Add olive oil into a medium pot. Add remaining garlic, onion and bay leaf and sauté until onions become translucent. Place seasoned chicken in the pot and brown a little. Add tomato paste, tomatoes, carrots, parsley and wine / beer used to flavor chicken. Bring to a boil and cook for a few minutes. Then add water so that it covers the chicken. Season with salt and pepper. Cook until chicken is done and carrots become tender.

If you want to serve spaghetti with the stewed chicken, add spaghetti and more water to the pot. As spaghetti is cooking, if the sauce starts to dry up, add a little more water. When making stewed chicken with spaghetti, be sure to serve immediately as pasta will soak up the sauce and cause it to dry up.

One type of food that screams comfort is a good homemade stew. In Portuguese, a stew that includes a combination of carrots, peas, potatoes, etc. and some type of meat / chicken is referred as a "Jardineira", thus the name of this dish. This particular Chicken Stew is a favorite of mine.

Chicken Stew with Peas and Potatoes / Galinha à Jardineira

Makes 6 to 8 servings

8 chicken thighs or legs
Salt and pepper to taste
½ cup olive oil
1 onion, minced
2 garlic cloves, minced
½ pound linguiça, cut into half round slices or cubes
2 bay leaves
½ cup white wine

5 cups water total or enough to cover, divided
3 medium tomatoes, peeled, seeded and cut into quarters
3 tablespoons tomato paste
2 carrots, peeled and diced
6 potatoes, peeled and cubed into 1 inch pieces
1½ pounds frozen peas
Dash hot sauce (optional)

....

Ahead of time, remove skin from chicken. Season chicken with salt and pepper to taste and set aside for at least 30 minutes.

Heat olive oil in a large stockpot. Add chicken and fry until the outside begins to turn a slightly golden color.

Add onion, garlic, linguiça and bay leaves. Move ingredients around with a wooden spoon so that these ingredients can sauté at the bottom of the pan. Sauté until onions become translucent. Add wine and two cups of water. Bring to a boil. Add tomatoes, tomato paste and carrots. Add salt and pepper to taste. Allow to cook for approximately 15 minutes or until tomatoes soften.

Next, add potatoes and frozen peas. Cover completely with water (approximately an additional 3 cups of water). Bring to a boil again and reduce heat to medium. If you so desire, add a dash of hot sauce. Cook for approximately 15 minutes covered, stirring occasionally. Remove cover, reduce heat and cook for another 15-20 minutes or until sauce thickens and all ingredients are fully cooked. You may also add the cover on partially if the peas look like they need to cook a little more. It is important to cook this dish uncovered towards the end so the sauce can reduce and thicken. This is when all of the delicious flavors are released.

A "Cozido" (Portuguese Boiled Dinner) makes a great Sunday family lunch. My mom made it often and would save the broth to make a hearty, delicious soup, which lasted for days. To the broth, she would simply add some collard greens and / or cabbage, chickpeas and spaghetti. This, of course, was a great way to get a few meals out of essentially the same dish.

Boiled Dinner / Cozido à Portuguesa

Makes 8 to 10 servings

1 to 2 pounds pork ribs
1 to 2 pounds beef ribs
Water, enough to cover
Salt to taste
1 linguiça sausage
1 farinheira sausage
1 chouriço sausage

1 morcela sausage
4 turnips, peeled and cut in half
1 head of cabbage, cored and cut into quarters
6 carrots, peeled and cut in half
8 potatoes. peeled and cut in half
2 cups long grain white rice

In an extra large pot, add pork and beef ribs with enough water to cover. Bring to a boil, add salt to taste and then reduce to low medium heat. After approximately 20 minutes, add linguiça, farinheira, chouriço and morcela sausages making sure there is enough water to cover. (Poke a few holes in farinheira and morcela with a toothpick to keep from bursting while boiling. Also, you may skim off some of foam / fat from meats that floats to top of pan).

When sausages are cooked, remove from pan and add turnips, cabbage and carrots. If there is enough room in pan, after approximately 30 minutes, add potatoes bringing to a boil and then reduce heat, allowing to cook on medium until all vegetables are tender. Be careful not to overcook potatoes. If there is not enough room in the pot, in a separate pot, add a little water with some of the meat broth and cook potatoes.

In the meantime, in a separate medium saucepan, cook rice according to package instructions and season with salt to taste. You may also add a little broth from the meats. When rice is cooked, place in a serving tray.

When meat and all vegetables are cooked and tender, carefully remove the meat and vegetables and place in a large serving tray or into separate trays. The sausages should be cut into individual serving sizes, approximately 3 inches long.

Note: There are various types of beef and pork that can be used in the cozido. such as pork shoulder or beef chuck roast. Also, chicken and / or slabs of bacon can be added. In addition, you can save the broth from cooking meats and vegetables to make a Cozido Soup. Simply add some chickpeas, cabbage and / or collard greens and spaghetti cut in half for a delicious, tasty soup.

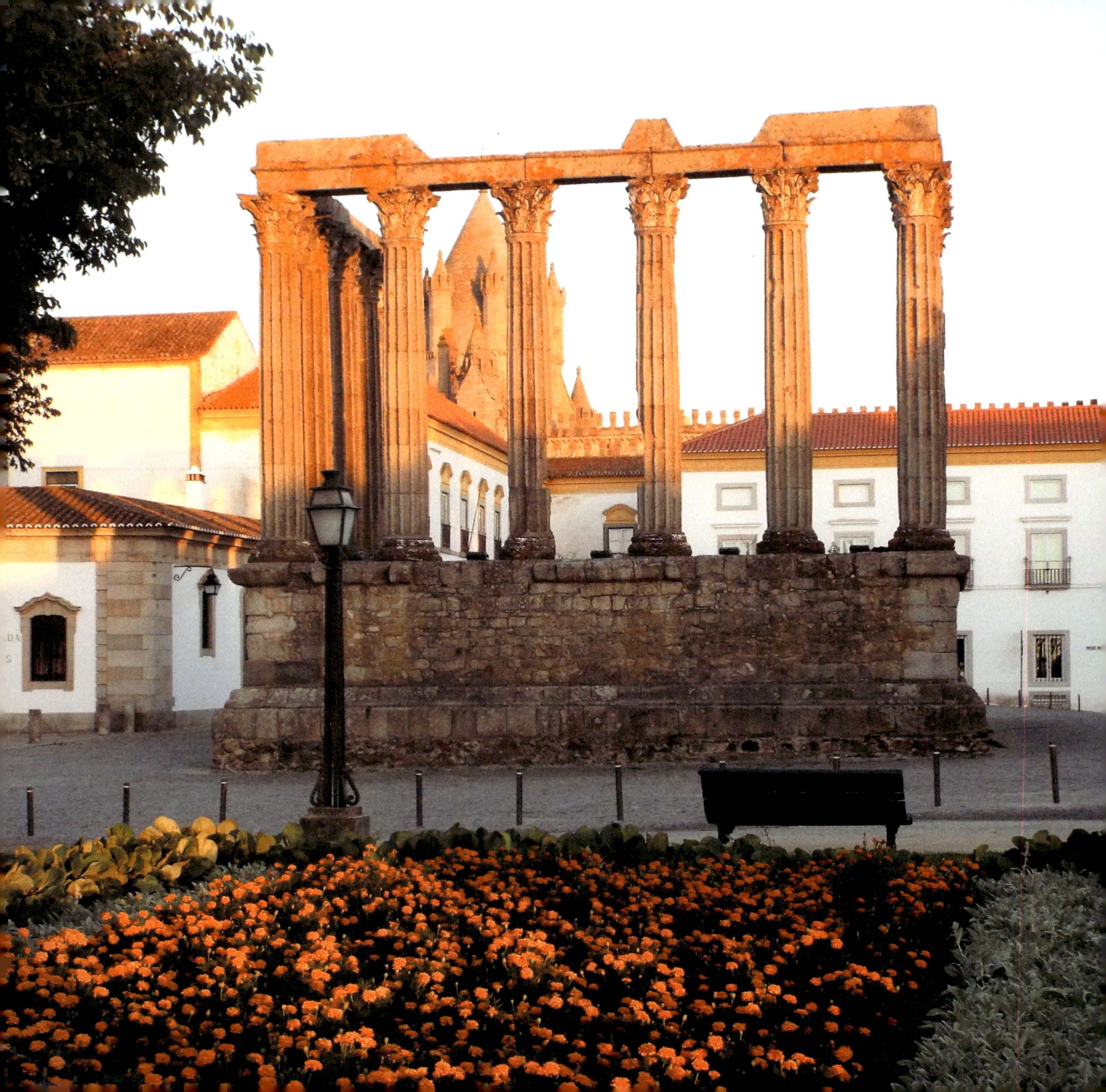

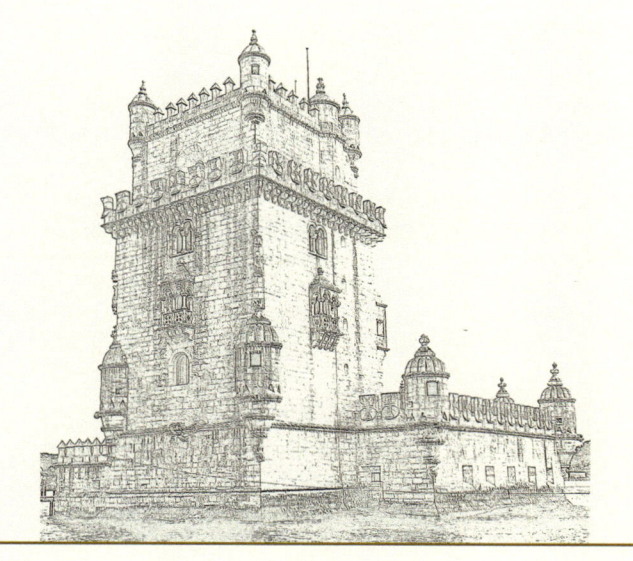

Other / Diversos

- Cannellini Bean Stew / Feijoada
- Fava Bean Stew / Favas Guisadas
- Red Kidney Bean Stew / Feijão Guisado

A very typical dish from the Porto region is "Tripas À Moda do Porto" or "Dobrada" (Tripe and Bean Stew). This is a very flavorful dish made with white beans and various meats including tripe. Personally, I prefer to leave out the tripe so I do not include it in my recipe, and therefore, it's simply called "Feijoada" (Bean Stew). Typically, this dish is served with a side of white rice and some fresh "Papo Secos" to soak up the sauce, which is extremely delicious!!

You can certainly include the tripe if you like. I would use approximately one pound of tripe cut into 1" cubes. Be sure to clean the tripe very well and boil it separately first before adding it to the bean stew along with the other meats.

Cannellini Bean Stew / Feijoada

Makes 10 to 12 servings

1.5 pounds pork shoulder cuts with bone or ham hocks
¼ cup olive oil
½ pound linguiça, sliced crosswise about ¼" thick, cut in half or quartered
½ pound chouriço mouro (blood sausage), sliced crosswise about ¼" thick, cut in half
2 bay leaves
2 onions, minced
2 garlic cloves, minced

4 tablespoons tomato paste
½ cup beer
6 cups water, divided
4 ripe tomatoes, peeled and seeded
2 carrots, sliced crosswise
½ pound salt pork, cut into cubed bite size pieces
Salt and pepper to taste
8 cans (15.5 ounces) cannellini beans, rinsed
Dash of piri piri or hot sauce

....

In a small pot, add pork shoulder cuts / ham hocks and enough water to cover meat. Season with salt and cook over medium heat for approximate 20-30 minutes. Once cooked, allow to cool, remove and then cut into cubes and set aside - saving only the meat and one of the larger bones. Discard the other bones and most of the fat if there is too much of it.

Heat olive oil in a large separate pot. Add linguiça, blood sausage and bay leaves. Allow meats to brown. Add onions and garlic until onions become translucent. Next, add tomato paste and beer and blend well. Add 2 cups of water. Bring to a boil and add tomatoes, carrots, salt pork, salt and pepper. Cover the pot and cook on medium until tomatoes and carrots start to become tender, approximately 20-30 minutes.

Once carrots / tomatoes are tender, add pork shoulder / ham hock cubed meat along with one of the larger bones. Add an additional four cups of water, cannellini beans, a dash of piri piri sauce and bring to a boil. Once boiling, reduce heat and cook on low medium covered for approximately 30-45 minutes. Remove lid and simmer until sauce thickens without drying out too much. At any point, if sauce dries out excessively, add a little more water and simmer some more.

Note: If the blood sausage is very moist / wet, I recommend letting it air dry for at least 24 hours. If sausage is too wet, it tends to fall apart when cooking in the stew.

Fava Bean Stew / Favas Guisadas

Makes 4 servings

- ¼ cup olive oil
- ½ pound linguiça or chouriço sausage
- 1 large onion, chopped
- 2 garlic cloves, minced
- 1 bay leaf
- 3 tablespoons tomato paste
- ½ cup beer
- 2 cups water
- 1½ to 2 pounds frozen fava beans
- 1 teaspoon hot crushed pepper sauce ("pimenta moida")
- Salt and pepper to taste

....

In a medium saucepan, heat olive oil and add linguiça / chouriço. Cook until slightly browned. Add onion, garlic and bay leaf. Sauté until onion is translucent and soft. Add tomato paste and mix well into other ingredients. Next add beer. Bring to a quick boil, and then add water. Allow to simmer for about 30 minutes uncovered.

Add frozen fava beans and again bring to a boil. Add hot crushed pepper sauce and salt and pepper to taste. Cover saucepan and allow to simmer on low / medium heat until fava beans are cooked, and sauce thickens. If at any time, sauce dries out too much, simply add a little more water and simmer a little more until sauce thickens again.

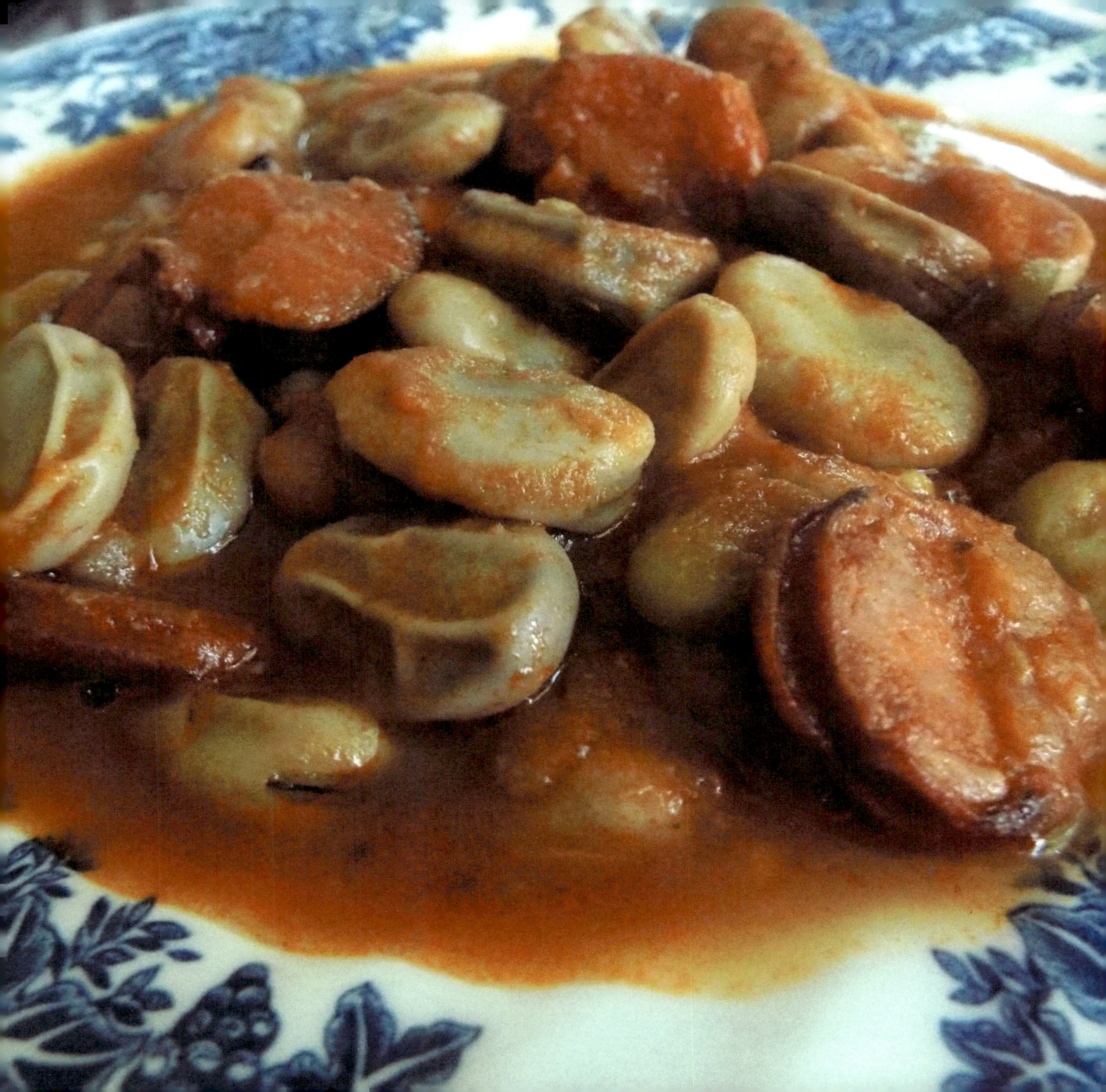

This is one of my favorite weekday "go to" dishes. It's very simple and quick to make. This stew tastes delicious with white rice or a simple side salad. Also, my mom always toasted some bread for dipping in the sauce, which is very tasty!

Red Kidney Bean Stew / Feijão Guisado

Makes 4 servings

4 tablespoons olive oil
½ pound linguiça, cut into ¼" round slices
1 bay leaf
1 onion, chopped
3 cloves garlic, sliced crosswise

3 teaspoons tomato paste
3 cups water
Salt and pepper to taste
3 cans (15.5 ounces) Red Kidney Beans

In a medium pot add olive oil, linguiça and bay leaf. Once the fat is rendered and linguiça slices start to brown, add onion and garlic.

When onion becomes translucent, add tomato paste and mix well with a wooden spoon and then add water.

Bring water to a boil. Add salt and pepper. Simmer until sauce starts to thicken a bit, approximately 30 minutes.

Add beans and cook over low heat for 45 minutes. If sauce dries out too much, add a little more water.

Can be served alone or with rice or salad. Also, toasted bread goes well with this dish for soaking up the sauce.

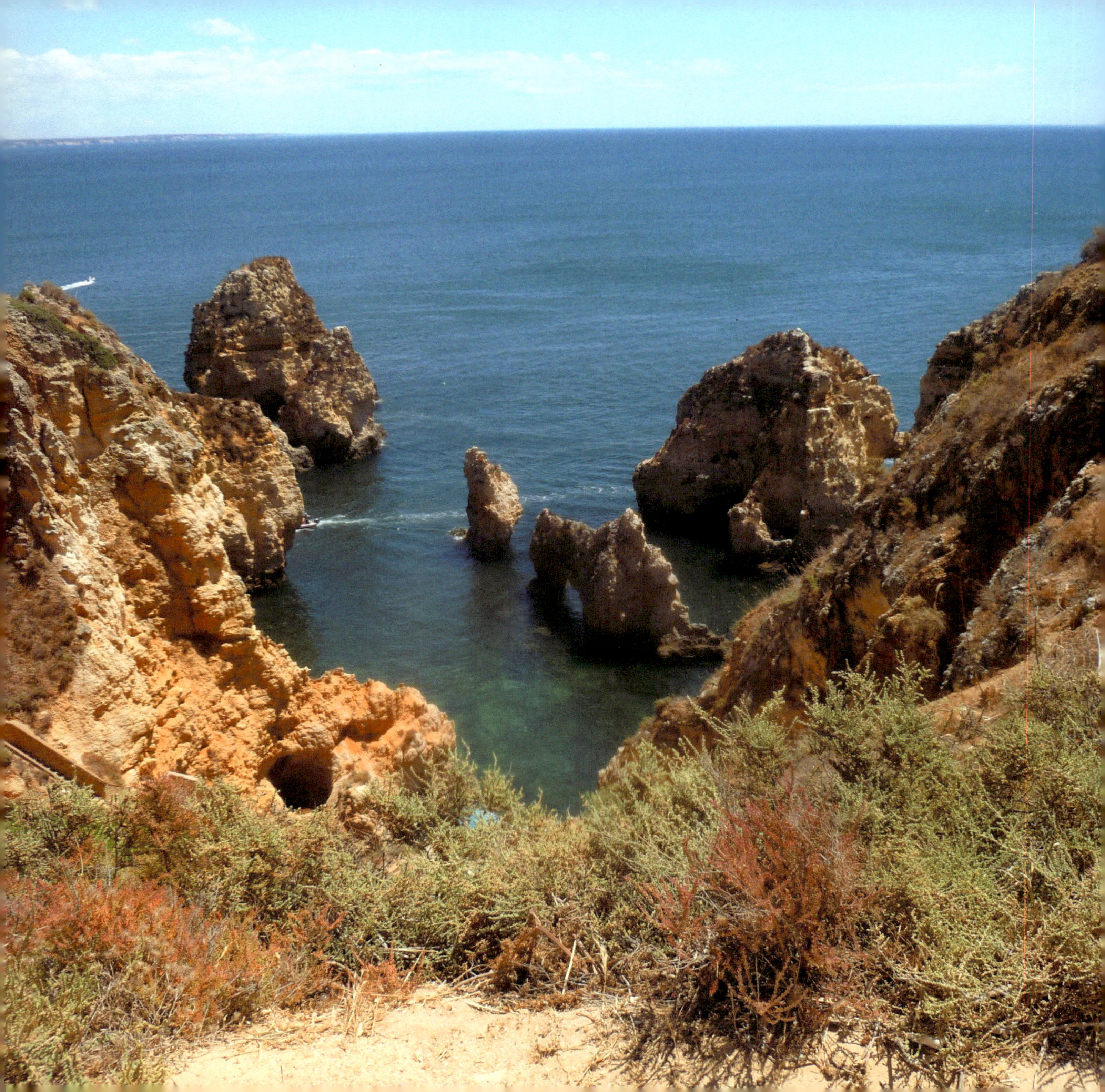

Side Dishes / Acompanhamentos

- Punched Potatoes / Batata a Murro
- Stewed Peas with Poached Eggs / Ervilhas Guisadas com Ovos Escalfados
- Tomato Rice / Arroz de Tomate
- Roasted Paprika Potatoes / Batatas Assadas com Colorau
- Sauteed Kale or Collard Greens / Couves Salteadas
- Spicy Roasted Potatoes / Batatinhas Assadas
- Cornbread, Black-Eyed Peas & Greens Hash / Migas
- Homemade French Fries / Batata Frita Caseira
- Black-Eyed Peas Salad / Salada de Feijão Frade
- Roasted Pepper Salad / Salada de Pimentos Assados

Growing up in a Portuguese home meant eating a lot of potatoes. We ate them boiled, fried, baked, roasted and even punched. I love potatoes prepared any which way. They all taste good to me!

Punched Potatoes / Batata a Murro

Makes 4 servings

3 pounds small to medium gold potatoes
Coarse sea salt to taste
4 garlic cloves, minced

1 cup olive oil
1 sprig parsley, chopped

Preheat oven to 400 degrees F.

Wash potatoes well and dry them off with a paper towel. Poke a few holes in potatoes with a fork or make a small slice in each with a knife.

In a shallow metal tray, lay bed of sea salt. Place potatoes on top of salt and rub / sprinkle some of this sea salt over potatoes as well.

Bake in a 400 degree F preheated oven for approximately 45 minutes to an hour, or until potatoes are baked and turning golden.

In a frying pan, sauté minced garlic in olive oil for a few minutes and remove from heat. Be careful not to burn garlic.

When potatoes are done, remove from oven. While potatoes are still warm, but not too hot to handle, shake off any sea salt stuck to potatoes or use a paper towel to hold them and rub off most of salt.

On a flat surface, place dishcloth over each potato and then punch it. Once punched, place potatoes in a serving dish. Pour olive oil with garlic over potatoes and garnish with chopped parsley. Enjoy with fish or meat.

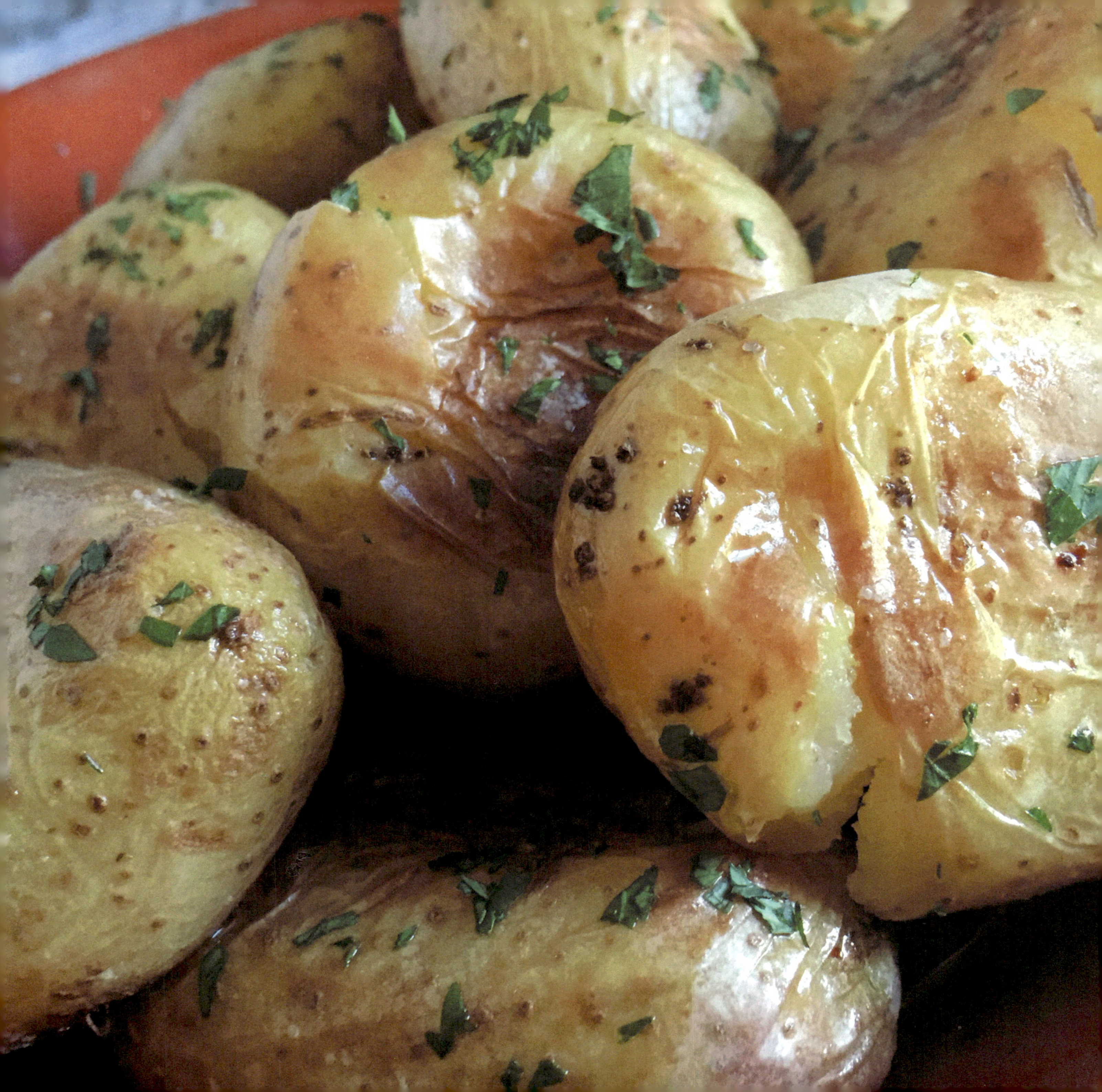

This is one of my favorite dishes / side dishes. We always make this as a side for Thanksgiving to add a little Portuguese touch to our Thanksgiving dinner. My sister, Linda, who passed away, was always in charge of making this dish on that day. She made it best! Stewed peas taste great with turkey and all the fixings. This is, however, a very traditional Portuguese dish and when served with poached eggs, it makes a meal in itself.

Stewed Peas with Poached Eggs / Ervilhas Guisadas com Ovos Escalfados

Makes 4 servings

¼ cup olive oil
½ pound linguiça or chouriço sausage
1 medium onion, chopped
2 garlic cloves, minced
1 bay leaf
3 teaspoons tomato paste
¼ cup white wine

1 pound frozen sweet peas
1 carrot, cut into thin round slices (optional)
Water, enough to cover
Salt and pepper to taste
Dash hot sauce
4 eggs

....

In a medium saucepan, heat olive oil and add linguiça / chouriço. Cook until slightly browned. Add onion, garlic and bay leaf until onion is translucent and soft. Add tomato paste and mix well into other ingredients. Next add wine. Bring to a boil.

Add frozen peas and carrots. Add enough water to cover (between 2 - 3 cups) and bring to a boil again. Add salt and pepper to taste and dash of hot sauce. Allow to simmer on low / medium heat until peas are cooked and carrots are soft and tender.

With a wooden spoon, create four hollows in peas, and break each egg into each hollow. Cover and simmer until eggs are cooked to your liking. At the very end, remove cover and allow sauce to thicken a little. It should not be too watery.

These peas can be served as a meal in itself or as a side dish with roasted turkey, chicken or pot roast. The poached eggs may also be omitted.

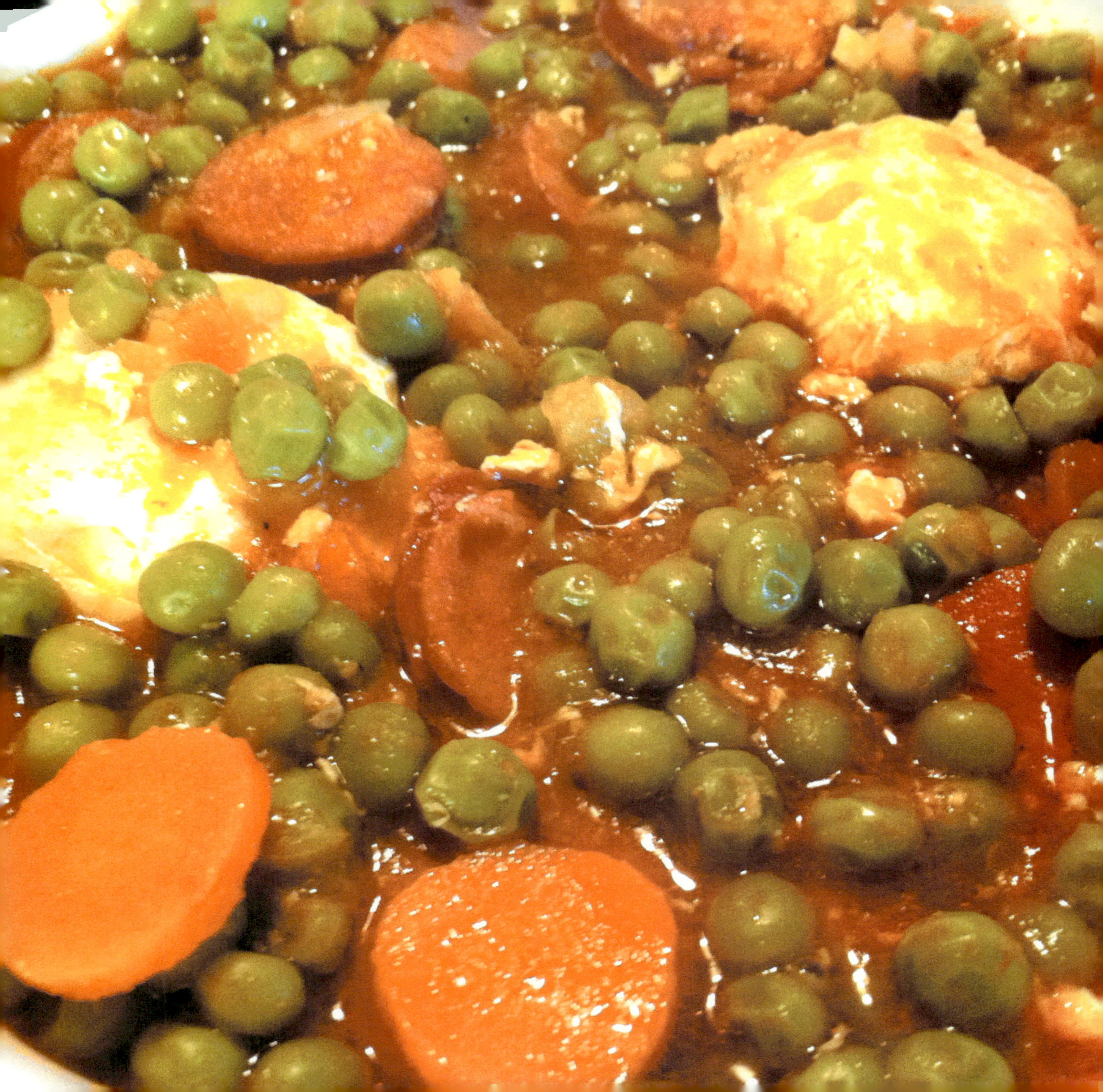

Tomato Rice has always been a favorite of mine. My parents made it often to eat as a side with fried fish and a salad. The three tasted just perfect together! Tomato rice is often served "malandro" style, which means wet and soupy and that's just how we had it at home.

Tomato Rice / Arroz de Tomate

Makes 4 to 6 servings

⅓ cup olive oil
1 large onion, chopped
2 garlic cloves, minced
1 bay leaf
2 teaspoons tomato paste

2 ½ cups of water, divided
2 tomatoes, peeled, chopped and seeded
Salt and pepper to taste
1 cup long grain rice

....

Heat olive oil in a medium saucepan. Add onion, garlic and bay leaf until onion becomes translucent and soft.

Add tomato paste and blend well with onions. Add about half of water and bring to a boil.

Add tomatoes and allow to simmer for about 15-20 minutes. Add salt and pepper to taste.

Add remaining water and bring to a boil.

Add rice and simmer covered until rice is cooked, approximately 20 minutes. If rice begins to dry up, add a little more water.

NOTE: This rice should be served "malandro", which means it should be served very wet / soupy. The rice should not be allowed to get dry. If it does, add more water and allow to cook a little more. Also, once cooked, tomato rice should be served immediately. Leftover tomato rice is still very good, but it will no longer be wet as rice will soak up the moisture.

Roasted Paprika Potatoes / Batatas Assadas com Colorau

Makes 6 to 8 servings

3 pounds medium Russet potatoes, peeled and cut into wedges
½ cup olive oil
½ cup white wine
1 teaspoon paprika

3 garlic cloves, minced
Salt and pepper to taste
2 bay leaves
1 sprig parsley, finely chopped

....

Preheat oven to 350 degrees F.

In a large bowl, add potatoes, olive oil, wine, paprika, garlic, salt and pepper. Mix well so that potatoes are evenly coated.

Place potatoes on metal baking tray, preferably in a single layer. Add bay leaves. Cover with aluminum foil and bake for 30 minutes.

After 30 minutes remove foil and increase temperature to 400 degrees F. Cook for an additional 10 - 15 minutes or until potatoes are golden and getting a little toasty. Turn potatoes at least once while baking.

Garnish with fresh chopped parsley.

Sauteed Kale or Collard Greens / Couves Salteadas

Makes 4 to 6 servings

1 bunch collard greens or kale
Salt to taste
4 garlic cloves, minced

2 tablespoons olive oil
Water
Pepper to taste

Wash collard greens and remove large stems. Coarsely cut greens into bite-sized strips / pieces.

Add collard greens or kale to a large stockpot of boiling water seasoned with salt. Cook greens for approximately 8 minutes or until they start to become tender. Drain greens in a colander.

Heat olive oil in a frying pan and sauté garlic for approximately 2 minutes, being careful not to burn it. Add collard greens to frying pan along with a few tablespoons of water. The water helps keep greens from browning / burning. Sauté greens for a several minutes in the olive oil and garlic until they become a bit wilted, tossing them around to absorb garlic flavor. You can also drizzle a little more olive oil onto greens while they are sautéing. Also, add salt and pepper to taste.

Spicy Roasted Potatoes / Batatinhas Assadas

Makes 6 to 8 servings

1 cup white wine
5 tablespoons of olive oil
3 garlic cloves, minced
2 teaspoons hot crushed pepper sauce
 ("pimenta moida")

2½ pounds small white potatoes, peeled
Salt and pepper to taste
1 tablespoon fresh parsley or dried parsley flakes
2 bay leaves, cut in half
2 teaspoons butter

....

Preheat oven to 400 degrees F.

In a large bowl, add wine, olive oil, garlic and hot crushed pepper sauce. Blend ingredients well. To this, add potatoes, coating them well with wine / olive oil mixture.

Place coated potatoes in an oven safe baking dish or metal baking tray. Pour wine / olive oil mixture over potatoes. Season with salt and pepper. Sprinkle parsley over potatoes. Other fresh or dried herbs, such as rosemary, thyme and terragon, may also be added. Toss potatoes around so that they are well-coated with parsley / other herbs.

Place bay leaves in baking dish with potatoes and add butter.

Bake at 400 degrees F for 1 hour and then increase to 425 for approximately 15 minutes or until potatoes are turning a golden, toasty color. Be sure to turn potatoes a couple of times while baking.

These taste great as a side to meat and chicken dishes.

Cornbread, Black-Eyed Peas & Greens Hash / Migas

Makes 6 to 8 servings

4 to 6 collard green leaves, coarsely cut into bite-sized pieces
3 (15.5 ounces) cans black-eyed peas, drained
½ Portuguese cornbread, crumbled

Olive oil
4 garlic cloves, minced
Salt and pepper to taste

....

Boil collard greens until tender. Drain when cooked. Also, give black-eyed peas a quick boil and drain.

Meanwhile, crumble cornbread into small pieces and fry in olive oil. You can choose to include or exclude crust, according to your personal preference. Once cornbread turns golden and looks a little toasty, remove from frying pan.

Add more olive oil to the same frying pan, and then add garlic. Sauté garlic until tender. Next, add drained black-eyed peas and kale leaves to pan. Add salt and pepper to taste. Next, add cornbread back into frying pan and mix well so that kale, cornbread and black-eyed peas are well mixed.

Note: You may substitute collard greens with other greens such as cabbage or turnip greens. Also, the original migas recipe does not include onions, but I do like to add them to my migas. If you choose to include onions, they should be chopped and fried in olive oil until translucent after you remove cornbread from frying pan and before adding garlic.

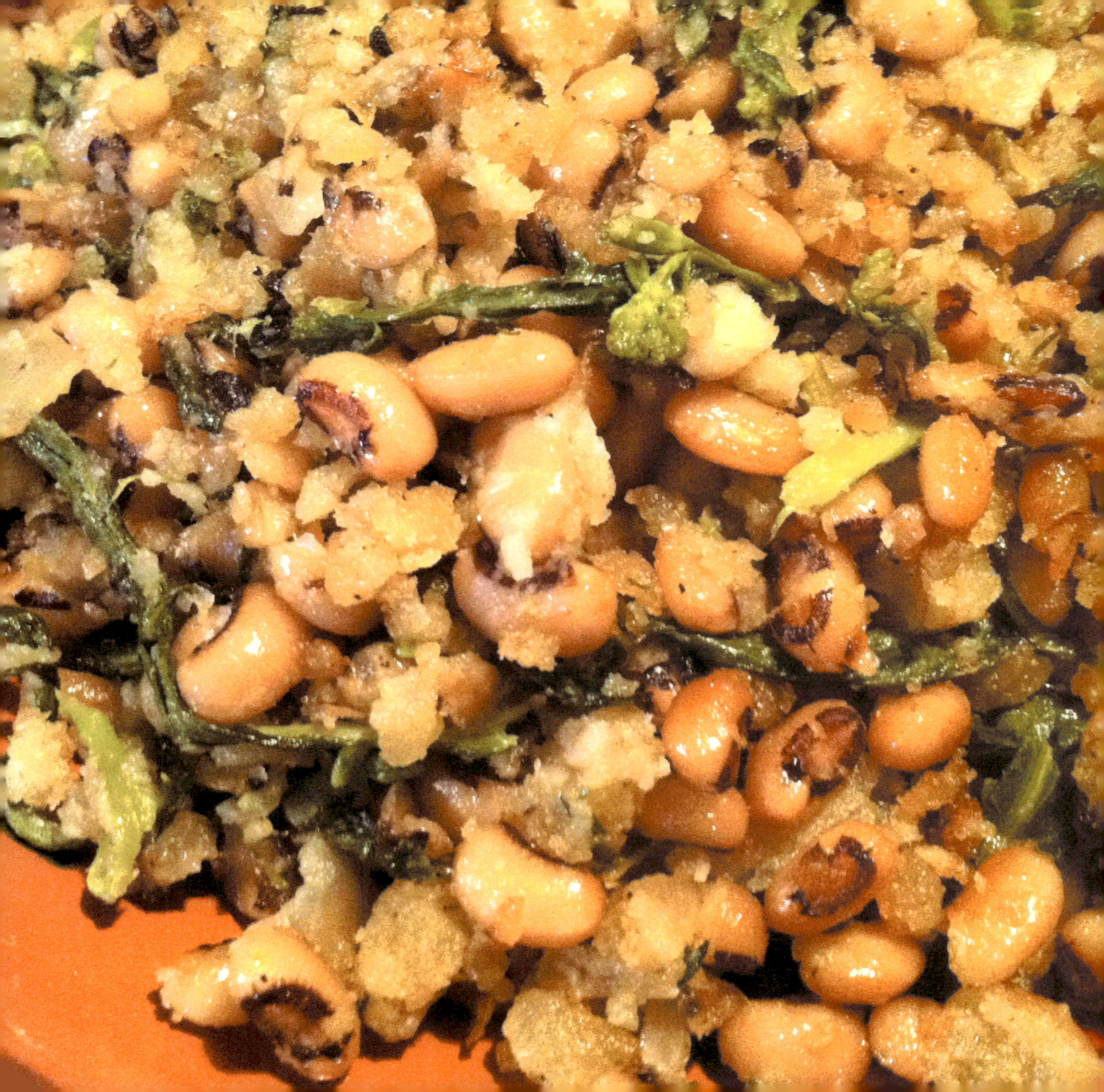

What can you say about homemade French Fries, other than, nothing compares. If I have one weakness, it's homemade fries. In the restaurants in Portugal, they are a side to many dishes, and it's one thing I just cannot resist.

Homemade French Fries / Batata Frita Caseira

Makes 4 to 6 servings

6 large Russet potatoes
Vegetable or canola oil

Salt to taste

Wash and peel potatoes. First cut potatoes into oval slices to your desired thickness. (Thin is best. I recommend no thicker than 1/3 of an inch). Then cut each oval slice into thin stick shapes.

Place cut potatoes in a bowl filled with water and rinse them well. You can leave them in the bowl of water with salt for 30 minutes to an hour or simply skip this step.

Before frying, place potato sticks on a paper towel to soak up much of the moisture and wetness before frying.

Pour oil into a large frying pan, enough oil to go about ¾" up the side of the pan and set to high heat. When oil is hot enough, add potatoes. Do not place too many in the pan at once. It is better to fry in batches. Turn fries once or twice with tongs to ensure that they fry well on all sides.

Once fries start turning a golden color, remove from the frying pan with tongs. Place on a flat dish lined with a paper towel to soak up the oil. Sprinkle with salt.

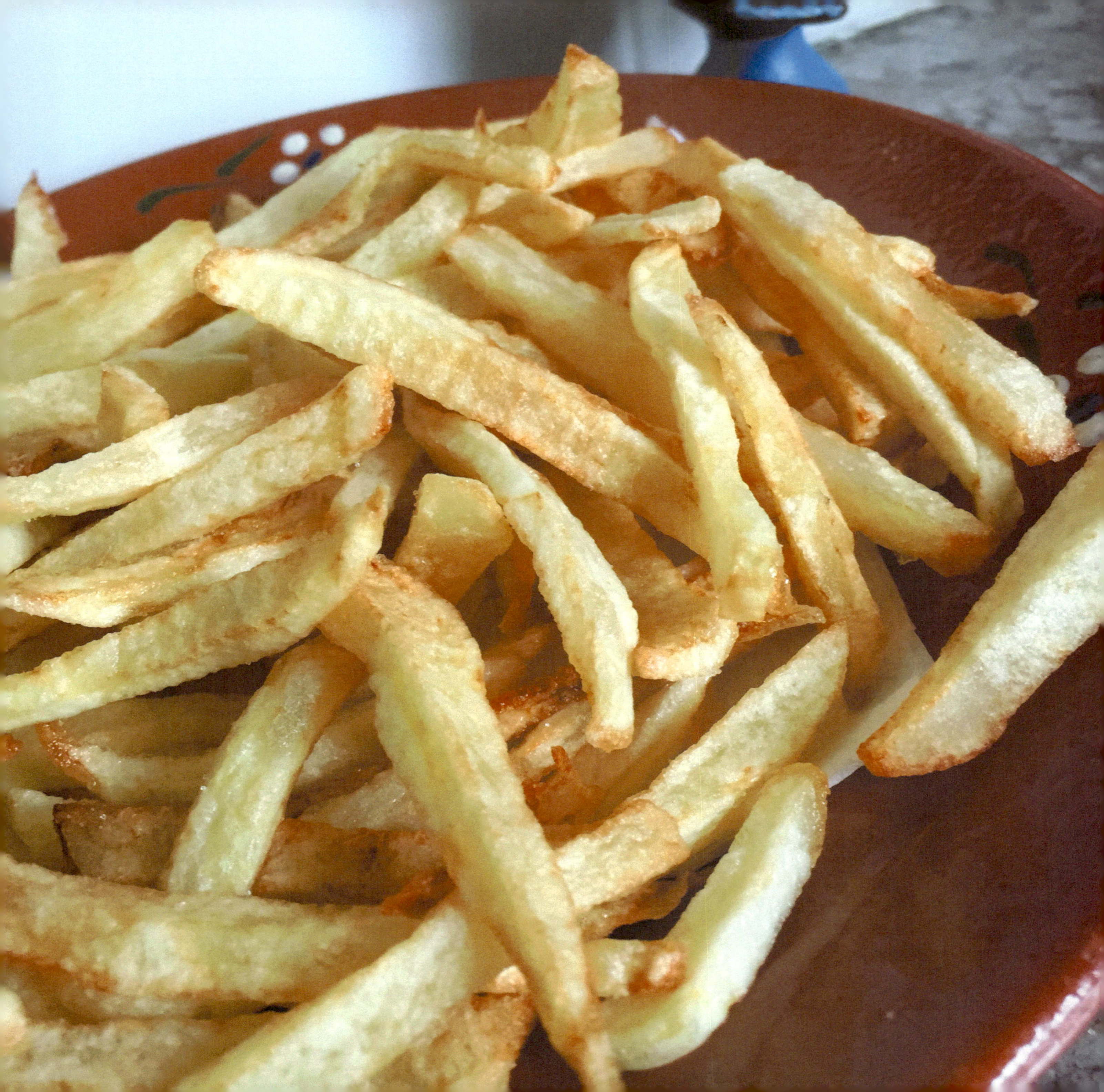

My parents made this often simply as a side dish for fish. When they wanted something other than potatoes, this was often what they made and what a good choice it was. I always loved it. Sometimes, they used chickpeas instead of black-eyed peas. You can also add tuna to make a meal out of it.

Black-Eyed Peas Salad / Salada de Feijão Frade

Makes 6 to 8 servings

2 cups black-eyed peas, cooked and drained
1 medium onion, finely chopped
5 tablespoons olive oil
3 tablespoons white wine or cider vinegar

2 tablespoons fresh parsley, chopped
Salt and pepper to taste
2 hard boiled eggs, sliced (optional)

If using dry black-eyed peas, soak and cook them per package instructions. Canned black-eyed peas may also be used. If so, drain, rinse and bring to a boil for a few minutes. Then allow them to cool.

In a serving bowl, add black-eyed peas, onions, olive oil, vinegar, parsley, and salt and pepper to taste. Mix well so that ingredients are well blended. Garnish with sliced hard-boiled eggs. Refrigerate for at least an hour. Serve cold as a side dish to fish or toss canned tuna into the salad for a meal.

This roasted pepper salad is a traditional and delicious side dish often served with grilled sardines.

Roasted Pepper Salad / Salada de Pimentos Assados

Makes 4 to 6 servings

3 red bell peppers, whole
3 green bell peppers, whole
1 medium onion, sliced thin crosswise
3 garlic cloves, minced

⅓ cup olive oil
⅓ cup vinegar
Sea salt and pepper to taste

Roast peppers on the grill or in the oven at 450 degrees F, turning occasionally so that peppers roast well on all sides and until they are a bit charred.

When peppers are roasted, remove from the grill or oven. Place peppers in a bowl, cover with plastic wrap and let sit for approximately 20 minutes. This allows peppers to steam, making it easier to remove skins.

Remove peppers from bowl. Peel, remove seeds and cut into thin strips. In the bowl, leave any liquid that was released from peppers as they were cooling off to use in the salad. Return pepper strips to bowl. Also, add onions, garlic, olive oil, vinegar, sea salt and pepper. Toss and blend all ingredients well.

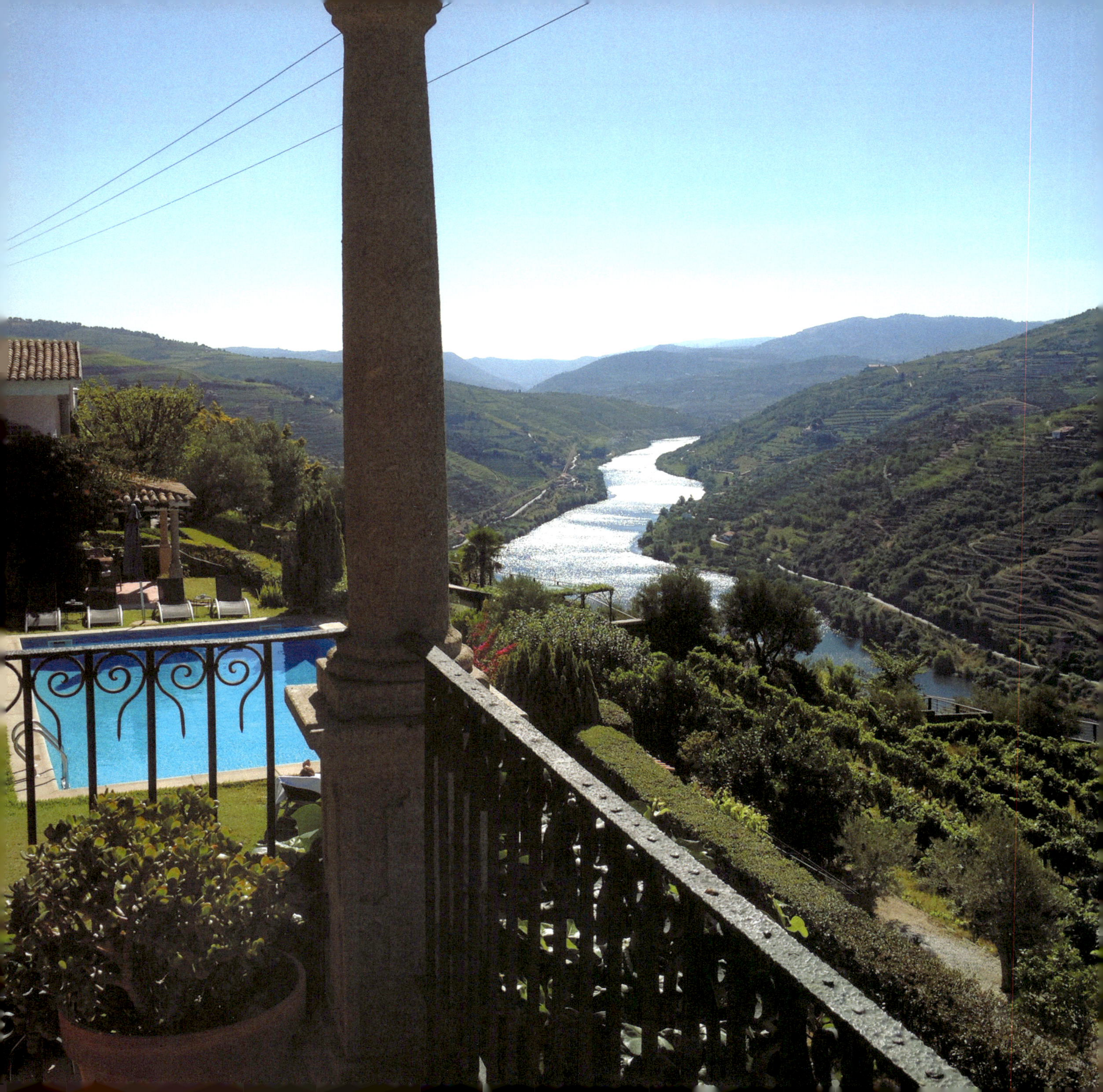

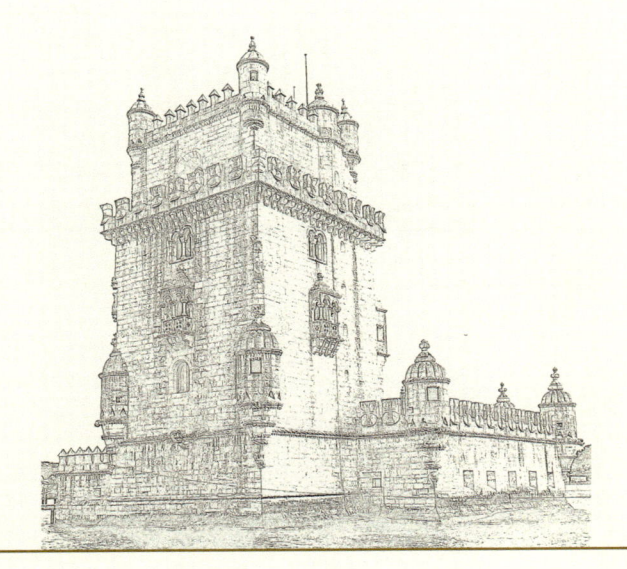

Desserts and Sweets / Sobremesas e Doces

- Portuguese Biscuits / Biscoitos
- Chocolate Mousse / Mousse de Chocolate
- Chocolate Salame / Salame de Chocolate
- Sweet Rice / Arroz Doce
- Layered Maria Biscuit Cake / Bolo de Bolacha
- Brazilian Flan Pudding / Pudim Flan Brasileiro
- Pineapple Mousse / Mousse de Ananas
- Heavy Cream and Maria Biscuit Layered Dessert / Serradura
- Portuguese Popovers / Cavacas
- Meringue Cookies / Suspiros
- Two Milk Custard with Meringue Topping / Doce de Dois Leites
- Meringue Souffle / Molotof
- Sweet Angel Hair Pasta / Aletria
- Portuguese Style French Toast / Fatias Douradas
- Almond Tart / Tarte de Amendoa
- Liquid Caramel / Caramelo Liquido

The list of delicious Portuguese desserts / sweets is endless. I admit, I inherited my dad's sweet tooth and so have my daughters. I like to have a little something sweet on a regularly basis with my coffee. When I say on a regular basis, I do mean every day, of course, but always in moderation. In this section, I have included some of the most popular and well-loved desserts. Many of which I grew up eating on a regular basis during holidays, birthdays and other special occasions. So many of these desserts bring back wonderful memories of growing up Portuguese. I think at one point or another in my life, almost every single one of these was at the top of my favorites list!

Portuguese Biscuits / Biscoitos

Makes 18 to 24 biscuits

¾ stick butter
¾ cup sugar
3 large eggs

3 cups flour
2 teaspoons baking powder

....

Preheat the oven to 350 degrees F. Lightly grease a cookie sheet.

Melt butter in the microwave or stovetop and allow to cool slightly. In a bowl, mix sugar and melted butter together well with a fork. Add eggs and blend well with fork or whisk.

In a separate bowl, add flour and baking powder and blend well.

Add flour mixture to sugar mixture and blend the ingredients together with a wooden spoon until dough starts to form. With your hands, work dough so that it is smooth and well incorporated. The dough should not stick to your hands. If it does, you may add a little more flour.

On the countertop or cutting board, knead dough for a little and then scoop out 1 heaping tablespoon of dough. Using your hands or countertop, roll each tablespoon of dough into a snake-like shape, approximately ½ inch wide and 5 to 6 inches long. Make a circle shape with dough, overlap the ends and pinch the two ends together.

Place biscuits on a cookie sheet. Bake in the oven for 20 minutes or until they start to turn a golden color.

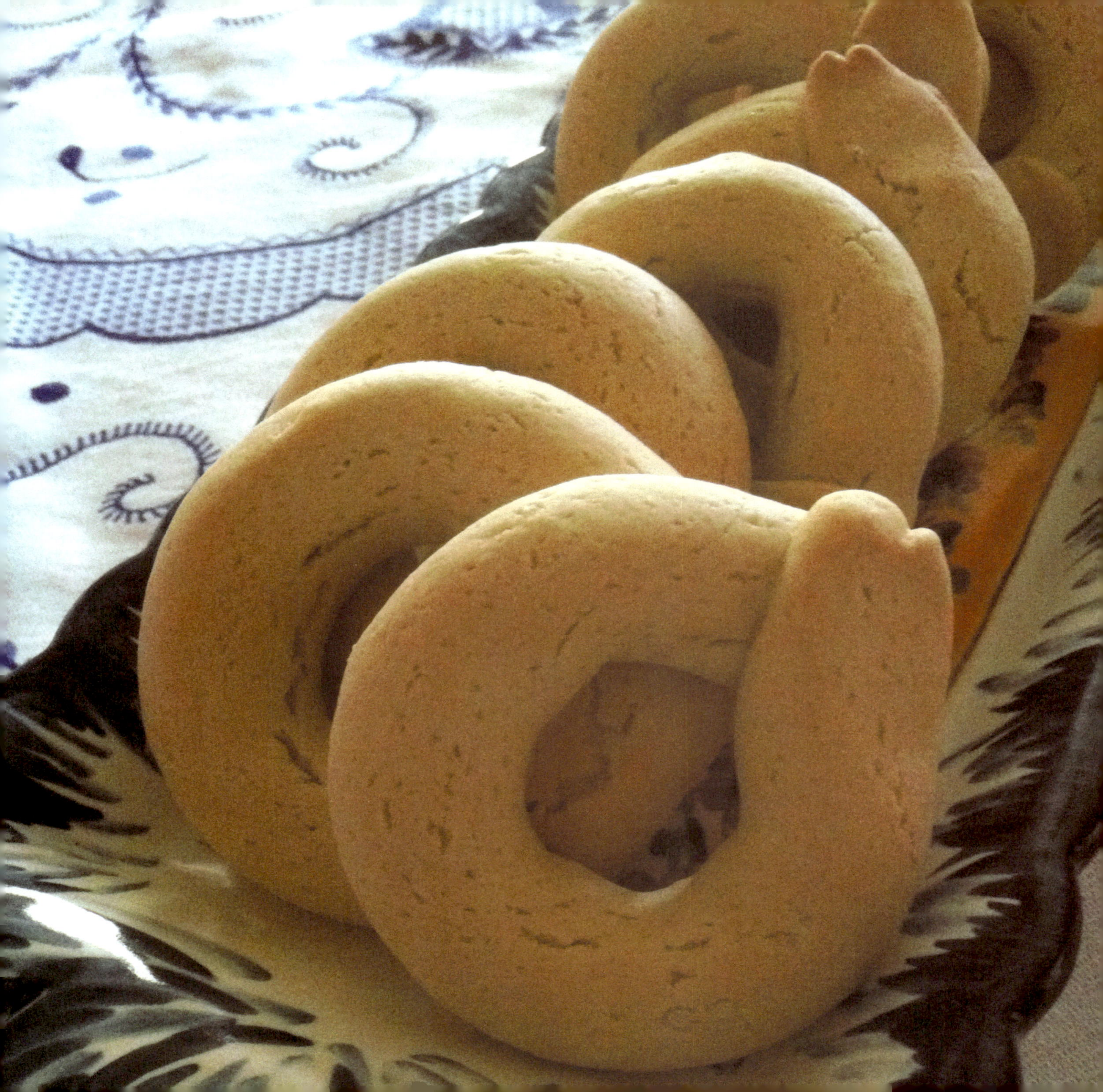

For as long as I can remember, my dessert of choice was always chocolate mousse, and it still is today. My one question when I order it at a restaurant is whether or not it is "caseiro", meaning homemade. For me to eat it, it must always be homemade.

Chocolate Mousse / Mousse de Chocolate

Makes 6 servings

1 semi-sweet baking chocolate bar (4 ounces)
6 tablespoons unsalted butter

6 large eggs
6 tablespoons sugar

....

Cut chocolate bar into pieces. Melt chocolate and butter together, either in a water bath / bain-marie on the stovetop or in the microwave. Be careful not to burn.

In a bowl, add egg yolks and sugar. Mix well with an electric mixer until it reaches a pale yellow, somewhat frothy consistency. Add melted chocolate / butter and blend well with a wooden spoon.

In another bowl, beat egg whites with an electric mixer until stiff, white peaks form. Be careful not to overbeat.

Gently fold egg whites into egg yolk / chocolate mixture until well blended, but do not overmix.

Pour chocolate mousse into a large bowl or separate individual serving dessert bowls and refrigerate for at least 3 hours.

Note: Because this dessert contains raw eggs, it should be stored in the refrigerator when not being served and should not be left out in the heat / sun for long periods of time.

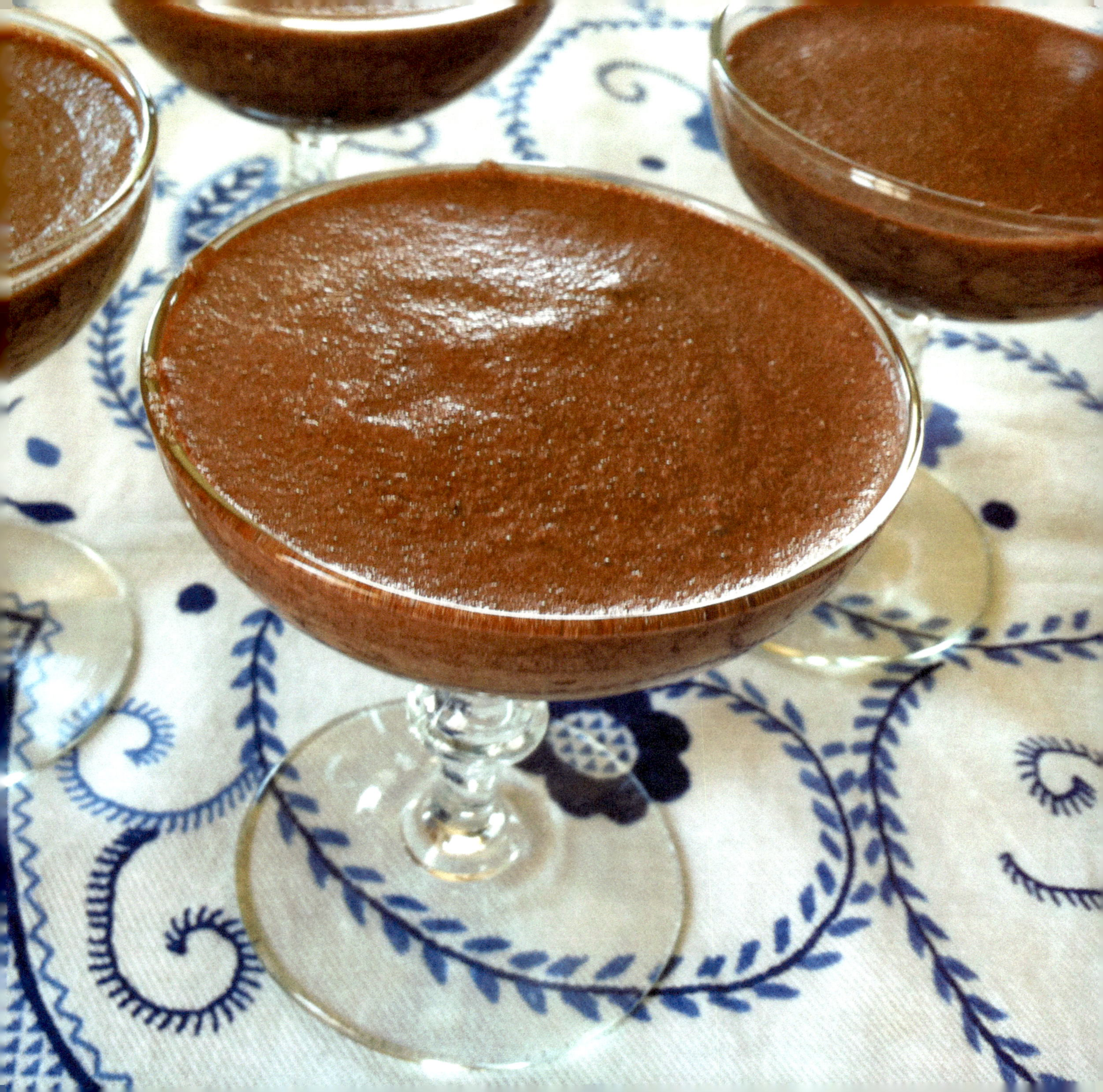

Maria Biscuits are a popular ingredient in several Portuguese sweets. These simple tea biscuits make any dessert taste delicious. Chocolate Salame, which is made with the popular Maria Biscuits, has always been a family favorite of ours. My mom always made it for every holiday or party. Today, I do the same. No holiday is complete without one of these on our dessert table because everyone in the family loves it!

Chocolate Salame / Salame de Chocolate

Makes 6 to 8 servings

1 package (7 ounces) Maria Biscuits
1 stick butter (equal to 8 tablespoons)
3 large egg yolks

5 tablespoons sugar
4 tablespoons cocoa powder
Sheet of wax paper approximately 12" long

Crush Maria biscuits into small bite-sized pieces. (You may crush / break with your hands or place in a plastic bag and smash with a meat tenderizer).

In a small pan, melt butter completely at a low temperature or in bain-marie (water bath).

In a bowl, add eggs yolks. To egg yolks, add sugar and blend well with a fork or whisk.

Next, add cocoa powder to egg / sugar mixture. Mix until ingredients are incorporated.

Add melted butter to mixture, blend well and then immediately add crushed Maria biscuits.

Use your hands to blend everything and then place mixture onto the wax paper and shape into a roll / log shape. Wrap the wax paper around the roll and squeeze tightly so that mixture holds.

Place roll in the refrigerator until it becomes firm (approximately 3 to 4 hours). When Chocolate Salame is firm, cut into slices about ½ inch thick.

Note: Because this dessert contains raw eggs, it should be stored in the refrigerator when not being served and should not be left out in the heat / sun for long periods of time.

There are a few different ways to make sweet rice. This recipe is typical of the region that my family is from. The milk is added slowly, resulting in a delicious, creamy, sweet rice. I have fond memories of watching my mom and sisters standing near the stove stirring the pot of sweet rice for almost an hour. My favorite part was always scraping the pan. The extra time and effort it takes to make this sweet rice is totally worth it. Also, in our sweet rice we do not add egg yolks.

Sweet Rice / Arroz Doce

Makes 2 trays / 6 to 8 servings each

10 cups hot milk
2 fresh lemon peels (about 3" long each)
4 tablespoons butter
1 cup medium grain white rice, rinsed

1 cup water
1 cup sugar
Ground cinnamon

Add milk and lemon peels into a large pan. Bring milk to a boil and then set heat to low.

In a separate pan, add water and butter. Bring to a boil. Add rice, reduce heat and cook until water is absorbed.

Transfer lemon rind in heated milk over to the pan with rice. Using a large serving spoon or soup ladle, begin adding heated milk to rice little by little and stir often. Continue to add large spoonfuls to rice, one by one, and allow to thicken slightly before adding another batch of heated milk. Continue doing this until all milk has been added to rice. This process takes approximately one hour. Stir often to make sure rice does not stick.

After adding the last batch of milk, add sugar to rice, bring rice to a boil and stir. Continue to simmer until rice and milk thicken to a consistency similar to that of oatmeal.

Remove lemon peels and pour sweet rice into two large, shallow serving trays.

Once cooled, pinch ground cinnamon between fingers and make the pattern of your choice on the sweet rice. Crisscross patterns are traditional.

Serve at room temperature and refrigerate the uneaten portion.

Here is another very popular and delicious dessert made with Maria Biscuits. Bolo de Bolacha is often served at restaurants throughout Portugal and a very beloved Portuguese dessert.

Layered Maria Biscuit Cake / Bolo de Bolacha

Makes 8 to 10 servings

2 packages (7 ounces each) Maria Biscuits
2 sticks plus 4 tablespoons butter, softened at room temperature
1 cup brown sugar
3 large egg yolks
1 cup strong coffee, cooled

Crush 4 or 5 Maria Biscuits and set aside to be used for topping.

Allow butter to soften at room temperature. (Do not melt in the microwave). Cut softened butter in squares. Place butter in a mixing bowl and add sugar.

With a wooden spoon, blend butter and sugar together so that butter softens a little more. Place in a mixer, add egg yolks and 3 tablespoons of coffee. Beat until the ingredients are well blended.

One by one, soak remaining Maria Biscuits in coffee. Be careful not to soak for too long, as they tend to fall apart if they absorb too much coffee.

Place soaked Maria Biscuits in a shallow dish or cake plate, so that they form the shape of a flower. (One Maria Biscuit goes in the center surrounded by six other cookies). On top of each layer of cookies, spread butter / sugar mixture. Be sure not to spread on too thick. Once you get to the last layer, use remaining butter / sugar mixture to frost the sides of the cake as well.

Sprinkle crushed Maria biscuits on top of butter spread on the last layer to finish off the cake.

Refrigerate for at least an hour before serving. Because this dessert contains raw eggs, it should be stored in the refrigerator when not being served and should not be left out in the heat / sun for long periods of time.

Note: Depending on how thickly the butter / sugar mixture is spread will determine how many layers the dessert will have. Stop making layers when running out of butter spread to make sure there is enough to cover the sides of the dessert. Some Maria Biscuits may be left over. Also, a couple of teaspoons of sugar can be added to coffee if desired.

Brazilian Flan Pudding / Pudim Flan Brasileiro

Makes 8 to 10 servings

1 cup sugar
5 large eggs
1 cup whole milk

1 can (14 ounces) sweetened condensed milk
1 cup water

....

Preheat oven to 350 degrees F.

Melt sugar in a heavy saucepan over low heat. Begin stirring constantly when sugar starts to caramelize and remove from stovetop when it becomes a golden, caramel color. Pour immediately into a flan pan, swirling the pan so that syrup coats all sides. Use oven mitts to handle flan pan when doing this, as it gets very hot to the touch. Set aside to cool for approximately 10 minutes.

In a bowl, whisk eggs until well blended.

Add milk, condensed milk and water to eggs and whisk again until all ingredients are well incorporated.

Pour mixture over cooled caramel in the flan pan.

Place the flan pan in a baking dish and fill the baking dish with boiling water so that it reaches about half way up the sides of the baking dish (referred to as "Bain Marie" or "Water Bath").

Place the baking dish in the oven and bake for approximately 1 hour or until the custard is set and firm to the touch.

Remove flan from the oven and allow to cool at room temperature. Cover and refrigerate until chilled, for a minimum of three hours.

Before serving, run a thin knife around the flan in the pan (around the top edge should be sufficient). Place a deep dish over the pan and quickly flip it over to unmold. If you would like more caramel over flan, simply add water into the flan pan after flan is removed. Swirl water around in the pan a bit and pour over flan in the dish or simply place the flan pan on stovetop to melt the hardened caramelized sugar and pour over flan.

Pineapple Mousse / Mousse de Ananas

Makes 6 to 8 servings

1 can (20 ounces) crushed pineapple
1 package (3 ounces) of pineapple gelatin powder
3 large egg whites

1 can (14 ounces) condensed milk
Pineapple slices to garnish

....

Place pineapple juice from canned crushed pineapple in a saucepan. Add pineapple gelatin powder and bring to a boil. Set aside to cool.

Beat egg whites in a mixer until soft peaks form.

When gelatin / juice mixture has cooled, place in a large bowl. To this, add sweetened condensed milk and crushed pineapple. Blend well with a wooden spoon. Fold egg whites into this mixture and mix slowly using a spatula until all ingredients are well blended. Place entire mixture into a deep serving dish and place in the refrigerator for a few hours.

Once mousse sets, garnish with pineapple slices.

Directly translated, "Serradura", means sawdust. The name comes from the fact that the finely crushed Maria Biscuits look like sawdust. This is the type of dessert that once you start eating, it's hard to stop. Serradura is a great dessert to make a day ahead.

Heavy Cream and Maria Biscuit Layered Dessert / Serradura

Makes 8 to 10 servings

1 package (7 ounces) Maria Biscuits, crushed to look like sawdust
6 large egg whites
1 pint heavy cream
1 can (14 ounces) sweetened condensed milk

Crush Maria Biscuits by placing in a freezer / food storage bag and pounding with a meat tenderizer / rolling pin or crush in a food processor. The biscuits should resemble sawdust when crushed.

Beat egg whites in a bowl until they start to form stiff peaks. In another bowl, beat heavy cream until it gets firm. Once heavy cream is firm, add in the condensed milk while continuing to beat until well blended. Fold heavy cream / condensed milk mixture into beaten egg whites. Beat until everything is well blended.

Put a light coating of crushed Maria Biscuits in the bottom of a glass bowl / container. Add a layer of egg / heavy cream / condensed milk mixture (half of the mixture). Next, add half of remaining crushed Maria Biscuits. Add remaining egg / heavy cream / condensed milk mixture. Top off with the rest of the crushed Maria Biscuits that is left.

Refrigerate for several hours before serving. Because this dessert contains raw eggs, it should be stored in the refrigerator when not being served and should not be left out in the heat / sun for long periods of time.

What can you say about cavacas? This a popular Portuguese sweet and one of my favorites that goes perfect with a good cup of coffee. What I like about these is that they really do not contain that much sugar. The batter contains no sugar at all. The only sugar used is in the icing used to coat the cavacas.

Portuguese Popovers / Cavacas

Makes 16 to 18 cavacas

10 large eggs, room temperature
2 cups sifted all-purpose flour

1 cup vegetable or canola oil

For sugar icing:
1 cup of confectioner's sugar, sifted
2 tablespoons of water

1 teaspoon lemon juice

Preheat the oven to 400 degrees F. Coat medium-sized muffin tins generously with cooking spray.

Add eggs into a large mixing bowl. Start beating eggs with an electric mixer on medium and slowly add sifted flour while beating. When well blended, add oil slowly while still beating. Continue to beat all ingredients together for 15 minutes.

Pour batter into muffin tins until ¾ full and place in the oven for approximately 30 - 40 minutes until a brownish golden color without opening the oven door. Opening the door may cause the cavacas to collapse.

To make the icing, in a small bowl, mix confectioner's sugar, water and lemon juice until it is well blended and reaches a thick consistency. If needed, add more sugar or water to get the consistency that you prefer.

After cavacas have cooled, drizzle with sugar icing. Allow icing to harden before serving.

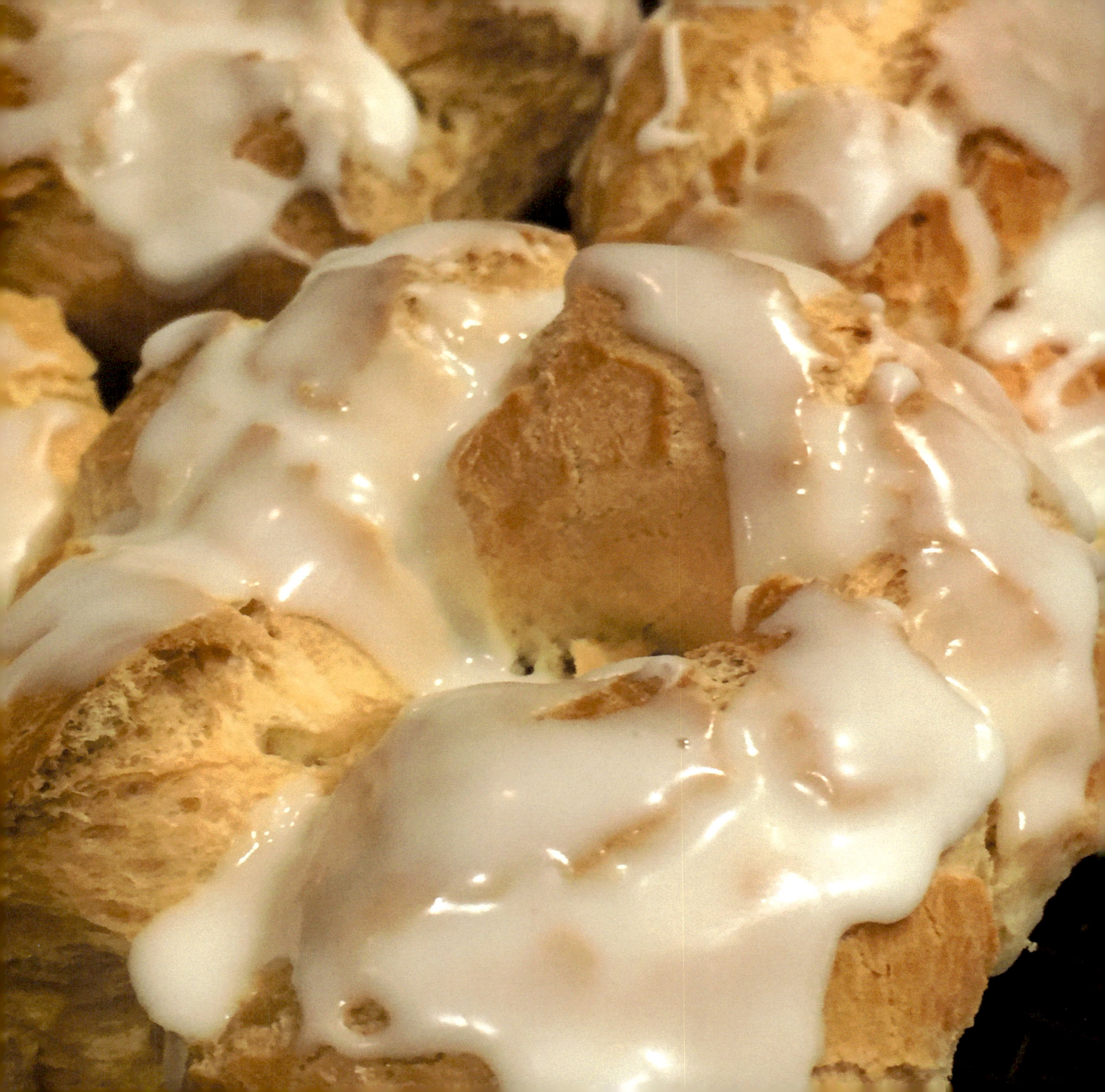

Suspiros were another sweet I loved growing up. They are a little crunchy on the outside and gooey on the inside. Directly translated, "suspiro" means "sigh". I assume it has to do with the fact that when people bite into them, that is just what they do: sigh.

Meringue Cookies / Suspiros

Makes 8 servings

3 large egg whites
1 cup sugar

½ teaspoon lemon juice (optional)

....

Preheat oven to 300 degrees.

Beat egg whites until soft peaks form. Then add sugar, one tablespoon at a time, and continue to beat until mixture forms stiff peaks. Add lemon juice.

Line a baking sheet with foil or parchment paper and add non-stick spray or coat with butter. Drop meringue mixture, one spoonful at a time, onto baking sheet. Allow enough space between each, as they will grow while baking.

Bake at 300 degrees F for approximately 20-30 minutes or until edges start to turn a light brown. Allow to cool completely on baking sheet before removing.

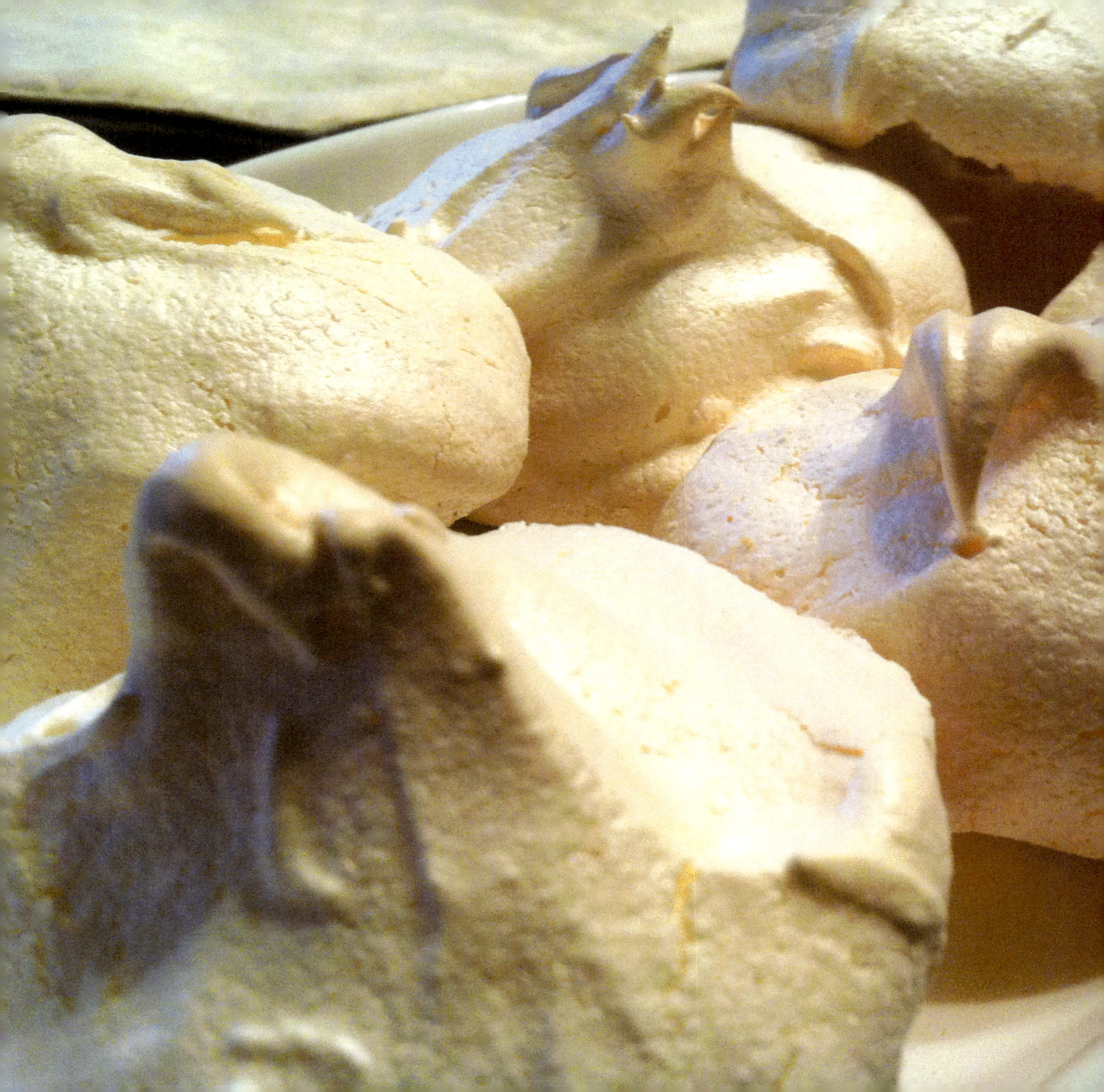

Two Milk Custard with Meringue Topping / Doce de Dois Leites

Makes 8 to 10 servings

½ cup sugar for caramel
4 cups milk
1 can (14 ounces) sweetened condensed milk
3 large egg yolks

4 tablespoons cornstarch
4 large egg whites
4 tablespoons sugar for meringue

....

Preheat oven to 350 degrees F.

Caramelize ½ cup of sugar in a small saucepan. When sugar turns an amber color and is in liquid form, pour immediately into an 8 " X 11.5" Pyrex.

In a medium saucepan, heat milk and bring to a boil. Then reduce heat. In a bowl, blend sweetened condensed milk, egg yolks and cornstarch well using a whisk, making sure there are no lumps. Pour condensed milk mixture into milk in the saucepan over medium heat and stir until mixture thickens. When it reaches a consistency similar to that of a custard, remove from heat and pour over caramelized sugar in the Pyrex.

In a mixing bowl, beat egg whites until stiff peaks form, adding sugar one spoonful at a time. Spoon egg whites over custard in the Pyrex and place in a preheated oven at 350 degrees F for 15-20 minutes or until egg whites turn a golden color.

Allow to cool and then place in the refrigerator for a few hours or overnight to chill. (Best when chilled overnight).

Meringue Souffle / Molotof

Makes 8 to 10 servings

10 large egg whites (at room temperature)
10 tablespoons sugar
2 teaspoons lemon juice

3 tablespoons liquid caramel (see page 123 for recipe)

For Sweetened Egg Yolks / Doce de Ovos:
6 large egg yolks
6 tablespoons sugar

3 tablespoons water

....

Coat the Bundt pan well with butter.

Preheat oven to 350 degrees F.

Beat egg whites with an electric mixer, slowly adding 1 tablespoon of sugar at a time. Then add the lemon juice while continuously beating.

When egg whites start to become stiffened, add liquid caramel, one tablespoon at a time while continuously beating. Continue to beat until egg whites are glossy and firm. The total beating time from beginning to end until egg whites reach the proper stage should be approximately 10-12 minutes.

Spoon beaten egg whites into Bundt pan, pressing them down well with a spatula and flattening them as you do so. Also, tap the Bundt pan on the counter to get any air out.

Place meringue in an oven safe tray and carefully add some boiling water into the tray ("Banho Maria" / "Maria Bath"). Allow meringue to bake for 10 minutes and then turn off the oven, leaving the meringue inside. Do not open the oven at any time. The meringue will continue to bake slowly even with the oven turned off. Allow meringue to stay in the oven until it returns to its original size (approximately 1.5 hours), and then remove from the oven. Note: While it is baking, meringue will rise to a much larger size, but as it slowly cools, it will begin to deflate. It will deflate until is gets to its original size at the time it was uncooked and placed in the oven. This is normal. After removing from oven, allow to cool completely outside of the oven.

In the meantime, make Doce de Ovos / Sweetened Egg Yolks to pour over molotof. In a small bowl, whisk egg yolks well and set aside. In a small saucepan, add sugar on high heat. After a couple of minutes, add 3 tablespoons of water and mix constantly. The mixture will get foamy. When it reaches a sort of runny, thickened consistency, remove from heat. Add a couple of tablespoons of sugar mixture to beaten egg yolks to warm them up and stir. Then add the all of eggs yolks to sugar mixture in the saucepan, mixing vigorously and continuously to blend well. Return to stovetop on low heat, stirring constantly until it slightly thickens. Set aside to cool.

When molotof has completely cooled, place a serving dish over the Bundt pan and flip quickly. Top molotof with the cooled, Sweetened Egg Yolks. Store in the refrigerator to chill. Can be served after a couple of hours in the refrigerator.

Sweet Angel Hair Pasta / Aletria

Makes 2 trays / 6 to 8 servings each

8 cups water
16 ounces angel hair pasta or Portuguese
    Aletria pasta
1 strip lemon peel (approximately 3 inches long)
1 teaspoon salt

1 tablespoon butter
5 cups milk
2 cups sugar
4 large egg yolks
Cinnamon to decorate

In a large pan, add water and bring to a boil. Add pasta, lemon peel, salt and butter. (If using actual Aletria pasta, before putting in the pan, break and separate the pasta a bit to keep it from sticking together when boiling). Cook for about 10-15 minutes or until pasta is cooked to your liking. Be sure to mix pasta well with a fork as it cooks, and using the fork, separate any pieces of pasta that are sticking together.

After pasta is cooked, add milk and bring to a boil. Add sugar and mix well again. (Note: if the pasta dries out too much or you like creamier Aletria, add more milk). Allow to simmer while stirring. Also be sure to remove lemon peel. When liquid becomes creamy and sticky, remove pan from heat and allow to cool for 2 minutes or so.

In a small, bowl beat egg yolks with a fork. Remove a few spoonfuls of cooked pasta and add to beaten egg yolks and mix well. (This warms the egg yolks before they are added to the pan so that they do not cook and became stringy / clumpy). Take egg yolk / pasta mixture and add to the large pot of cooked pasta. Mix everything well so egg yolks are well blended into pasta.

Pour Aletria in a shallow serving dish / platter and spread evenly.

After Aletria has cooled, sprinkle some ground cinnamon on top to decorate.

Note: This recipe makes two large platters of Aletria.

Some people call these Fatias Douradas or Fatias Paridas. Others call them Rabanadas. My mother simply called them Fatias. I have fond memories of my mom making Fatias with bread that was a few days old. In Portuguese fashion, nothing could ever go to waste, so this was something to do with bread that was going stale or no longer fresh. They were always a treat.

Portuguese Style French Toast / Fatias Douradas

Makes 6 to 8 servings

Portuguese Viana, French or Italian bread loaf (preferably a few days old)
Canola or vegetable oil
4 large eggs
2 cups milk
Cinnamon and sugar to coat

....

Cut bread into slices about ¾" thick.

Heat oil in a large frying pan, adding just enough oil to fry the toast.

Whisk eggs in a bowl so that they are well mixed. In a separate bowl, add milk.

One by one, dip each bread slice in milk, allowing any excess milk to drip off. Next, dip bread in egg, allowing any excess egg to drip off as well, and then add to frying pan. (You will need to fry bread in batches).

Allow toast to fry, turning at least once so that it is golden brown on both sides. Remove and place on a flat dish lined with a paper towel to soak up excess oil.

Dip toasts in a sugar and cinnamon mixture to coat.

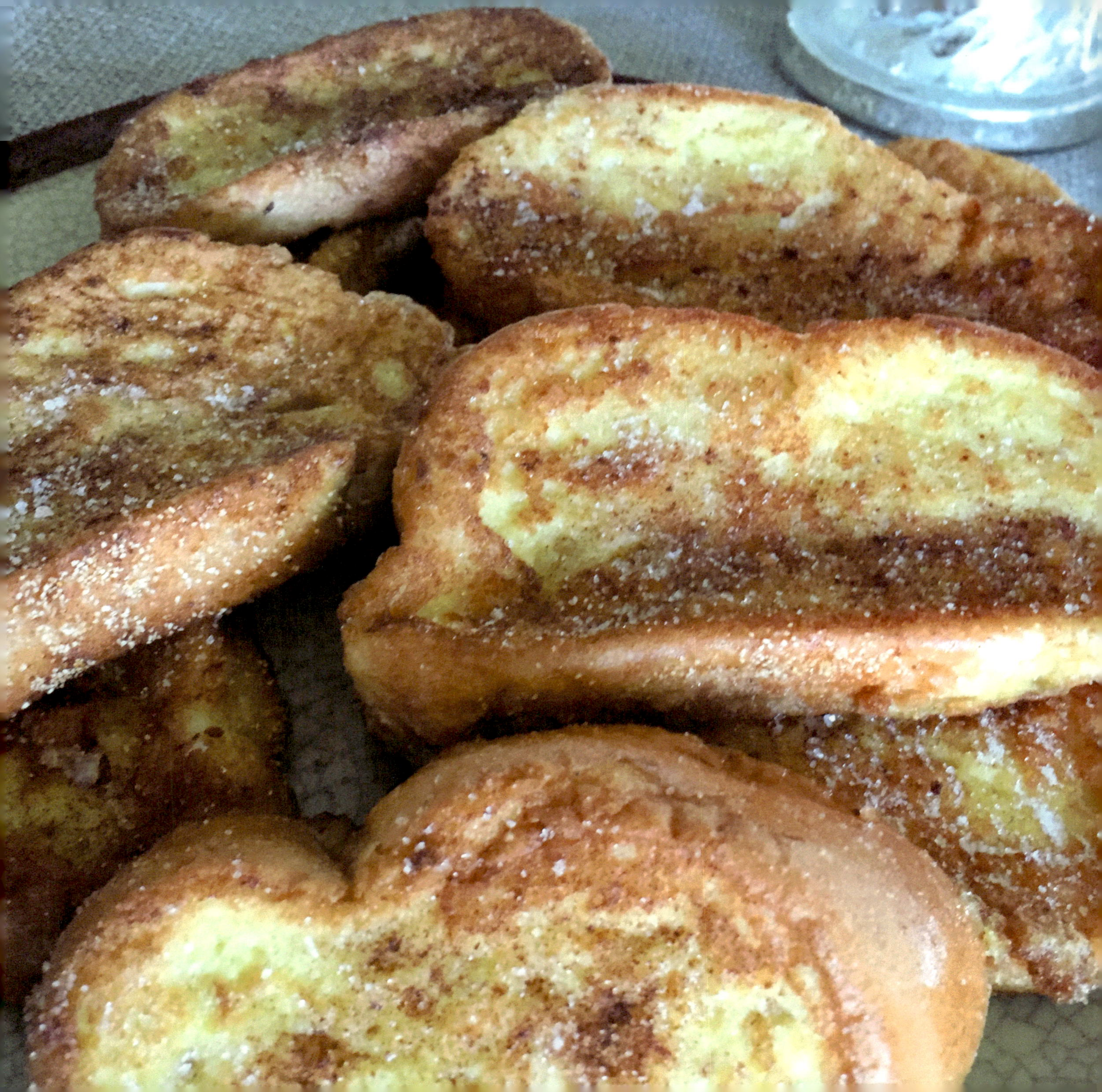

Almond Tart / Tarte de Amêndoa

Makes 10 to 12 servings

Filling:
1 stick butter, softened
1 cup sugar
2 large eggs, beaten
1 cup flour
Additional flour to coat tart pan

Topping:
½ cup sugar
1 stick butter
6 tablespoons milk
1 cup sliced almonds

....

Preheat over to 350 degrees F.

Filling:
Grease an 11" removable bottom tart pan with nonstick spray and sprinkle with flour. Cream butter with sugar. To this, add eggs and flour, mixing well. Spread mixture into tart tin and bake for about 20 minutes at 350 degrees F or until the center looks spongy and is golden. Remove from the oven and set aside.

Topping:
Mix sugar, butter, milk and almond slices in a saucepan. Heat mixture up until it starts to boil and turns into an opaque, tan color. Spread topping over cooked dough and return to the oven. Bake at 350 degrees F for at least 10 minutes or until topping turns a golden brown color. Allow to cool before serving.

When it is time to remove tart from the pan, it may be necessary to run a knife along edges to help release it.

Liquid Caramel / Caramelo Liquido

⅓ cup sugar
⅓ cup water

....

Heat sugar on medium / high heat in a small heavy-bottomed saucepan. Allow sugar to start melting into a liquid underneath and on sides of pan, and then begin to stir with a clean wooden spoon. As sugar lumps form while stirring, reduce heat and stir vigorously until lumps are dissolved, always being careful to not allow sugar to burn.

Once sugar melts completely into liquid form and is a golden amber color, immediately add water leaving on low heat. Be careful and stand back because when you do this, the water / sugar mixture will bubble and splatter. (Note: The melted sugar will harden when water is added). Let sugar incorporate into the water over low heat for a bit and then increase heat to medium / high. Once all of the sugar is incorporated into water and caramel is a clear amber liquid, immediately pour caramel into a heat safe dish carefully, being careful not burn yourself, as the melted sugar is very hot.

Allow liquid caramel to cool. It will thicken into a syrupy consistency and can be set aside to be used at a later time.

Be careful not to leave sugar on the stovetop too long as it could burn. Also, the longer you leave the sugar on the stovetop after adding the water, the thicker caramel sauce will be.

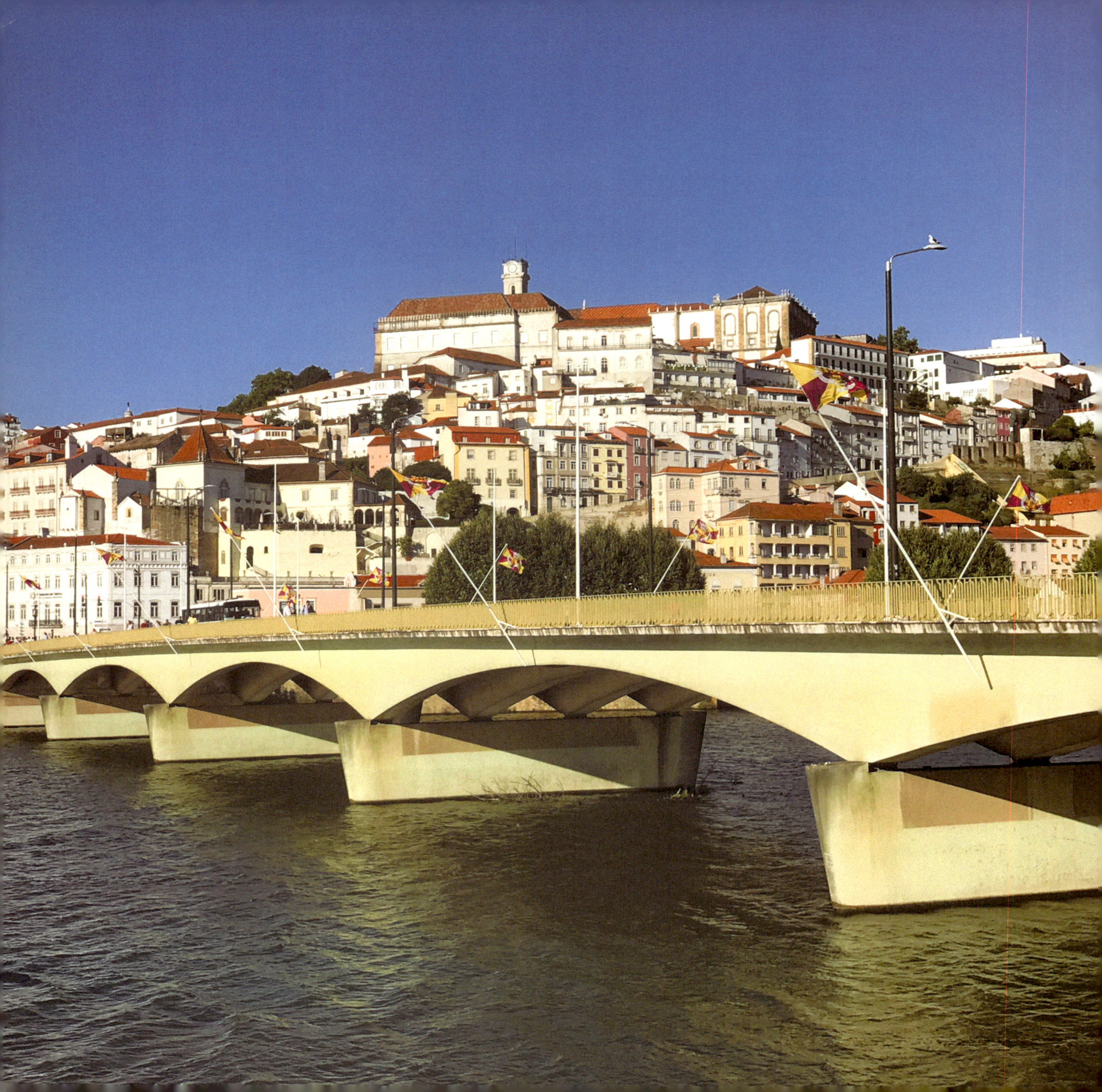

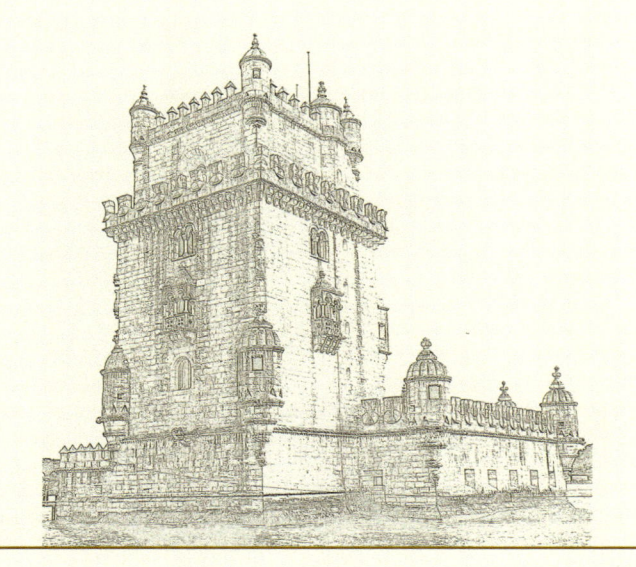

Bread / Pão

- Cornbread / Broa
- Meat Bread / Folar de Chaves
- Sweet Portuguese Easter Bread / Folar de Ovos
- Portuguese Bread Rolls / Papo Secos

Cornbread / Broa

Makes 10 to 12 servings

2 (¼ ounce) active dry yeast packets
½ cup warm water
2 teaspoons sugar
3 cups white corn flour

4 cups boiling water, divided
2 teaspoons salt
3 cups all-purpose flour

....

Add yeast and sugar to warm water and mix vigorously until yeast is completely dissolved. Set aside for 10 minutes to form a yeast foam.

In a large mixing bowl, add white corn flour and most of boiling water (more or less 3 cups), mixing with a wooden spoon until all of corn flour is moist. (Set remaining boiled water aside). At this time, dough will look lumpy. Set aside for about 5 minutes to cool. Once it is cool enough to handle, knead with hands to form a smooth dough. To this, add salt, yeast foam and then gradually add all-purpose flour. When gradually adding the flour, if more water is needed at any point, use water that was boiled earlier, which should be tepid at this point.

Knead all ingredients for approximately 10 minutes to form a smooth dough. At any point if dough is too sticky, add a little more all-purpose flour. Shape into a ball, place in a large bowl lined with a generous amount of all-purpose flour and sprinkle a little more flour on top. Set the bowl in a warm, draft-free place covered with a clean dish towel for approximately 60 minutes or until it rises to about double in size. As dough rises, cracks will form in the dough, which is normal with cornbread.

When dough is ready to bake, cut in half, being careful when handling so that dough does not deflate too much. Place the two pieces of dough on a well-floured cookie sheet. Cover with a clean dish towel, place in a warm draft-free place and allow to rise for approximately another 30 minutes.

Bake cornbread in a 500 degree F preheated oven for 30 minutes. After the 30 minutes, reduce heat to 350 degrees F and bake until cornbread turns a golden brown.

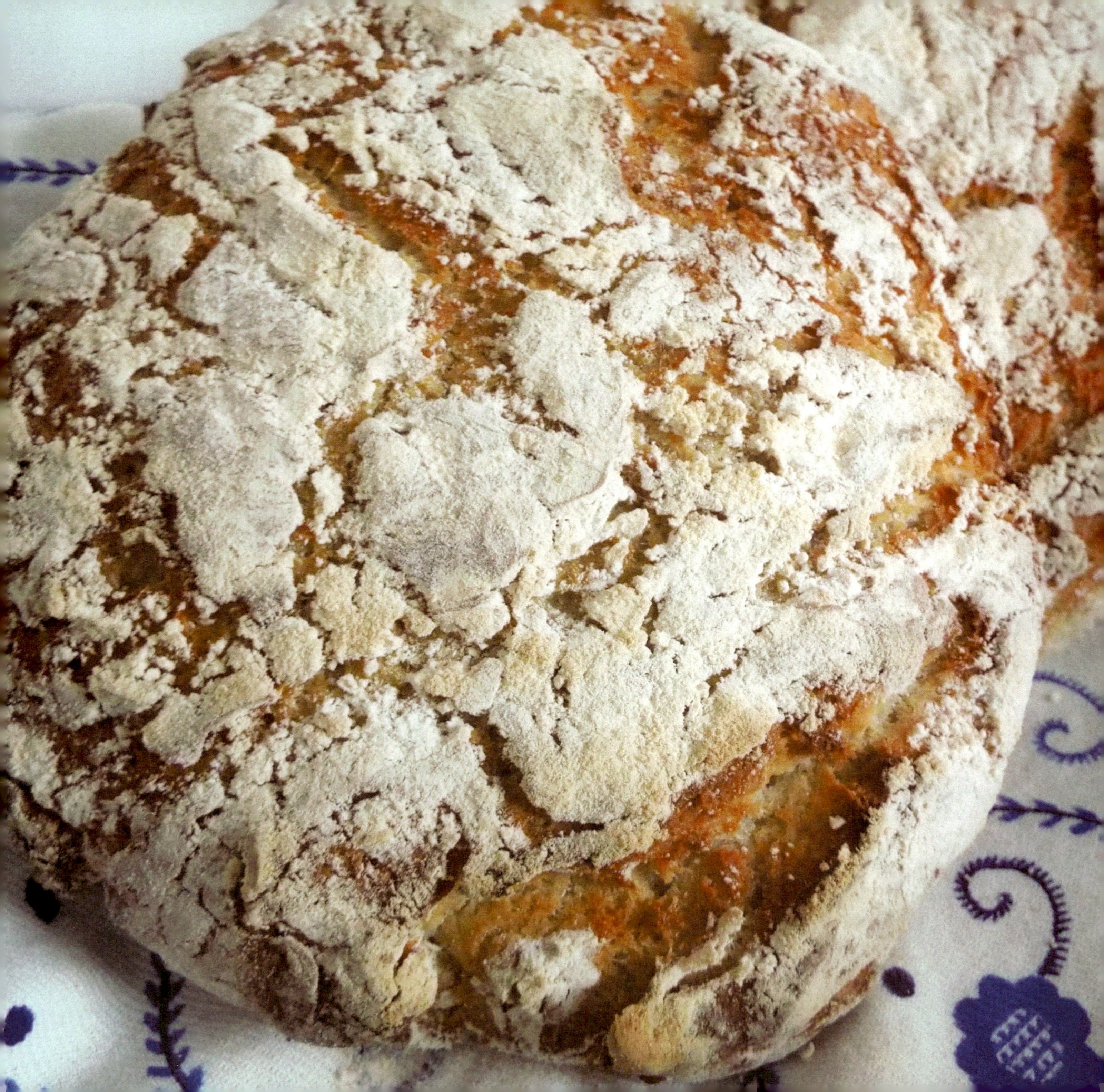

Meat Bread / Folar de Chaves

Makes 10 to 12 servings

2 (¼ ounce) active dry yeast packets
½ cup water
2 teaspoons sugar
1½ pounds salted pork / bacon slab
1½ pounds linguiça
6 tablespoons butter

½ cup olive oil
12 large eggs, room temperature
8 cups pre-sifted all-purpose flour
1 tablespoon salt
Olive oil to coat bread

....

Add yeast and sugar to warm water and mix vigorously until yeast is completely dissolved. Set aside for 10 minutes to form a yeast foam.

Remove thick skin from salted pork / bacon slab. Boil pork and linguiça in a saucepan for approximately 10 minutes. Remove from heat to cool. After cooled, remove meats from water, allow to dry and cut into bite-sized pieces. Set aside.

Heat butter and olive oil in a small saucepan until butter melts without overheating. Set aside.

In a medium bowl, whisk eggs. Also, set aside.

Add flour and salt into a separate, large bowl. When yeast foam is ready, make a well in the middle of flour, add yeast foam and blend into flour. Next, add eggs and blend mixture well with your hands. Slowly add warmed butter and olive oil, while blending into dough.

Transfer dough onto a clean, flat, floured surface and knead dough for 30 - 45 minutes until dough becomes soft, smooth and does not stick to hands. If at any point, dough is too sticky, add a little more flour, one tablespoon at a time.

Lightly coat a large bowl with flour. Shape dough into a large ball and place in the bowl. Dust dough with a little flour on top and make a cross sign in dough. Cover well with a large dishcloth and place in a warm, draft-free place for 2-3 hours.

After dough has doubled, cut dough into two equal sized pieces. Place each piece of dough on a clean, flat surface greased with olive oil and spread it out into a rectangular shape. Place half of the meat onto the laid out dough, making sure to cover all of the surface. Next, starting with the end closest to you, start rolling dough until a long roll is formed.

Coat a baking dish / Pyrex with olive oil and sprinkle lightly with flour. Place the rolled dough filled with meat into the baking dish, cover with a dishcloth and place in a warm, draft-free area for another 45 minutes to an hour.

Preheat oven to 350 degrees F. When ready, brush olive oil over dough and place into the oven for approximately one hour until bread turns a golden brown color.

Allow to cool for at least 15 minutes before removing from baking dish. May be served warm or cold.

NOTE: Instead of coating with olive oil, you may also coat with egg wash. To make egg wash, simply whisk two egg yolks.

Sweet Portuguese Easter Bread / Folar de Ovos

Makes 8 to 10 servings

2 active dry yeast ¼ ounce packets
½ cup warm milk
2 teaspoons sugar
8 cups all-purpose flour
1 pinch salt
2 cups sugar
8 large brown eggs, room temperature

1 stick butter softened at room temperature, cut into cubes
Peel of 1 lemon, grated
1 teaspoon cinnamon
1 teaspoon anise powder
2 hard boiled eggs
1 large egg, whisked (for egg wash)

....

Add yeast and sugar to warm milk and mix vigorously until yeast is completely dissolved. Set aside for 10 minutes to form a yeast foam.

Whisk eggs and set aside.

Mix flour and salt in a large bowl. To this, add yeast foam and then remaining ingredients: sugar, eggs, butter, grated lemon, cinnamon and anise powder. Blend all ingredients well and knead with hands for approximately 10 minutes. The dough should be soft, elastic and not too sticky. If it is very sticky, add more flour, just a little at a time.

Shape dough into a ball and place into a well-floured bowl. Cover with a dishcloth and place in a warm, non-drafty area for about 2 to 2.5 hours or until dough has almost doubled in size.

In the meantime, boil eggs that are to go on top of Easter Bread along with the skin of 2 onions. This will enhance the color of brown eggs.

Preheat oven to 425 degrees F. Butter and flour a cookie sheet or shallow metal baking tray.

Remove dough from the bowl after it has risen and place on a well-floured surface. Cut off approximately ½ cup of dough and set aside to use for cross decoration on top of bread.

Cut remaining dough in half and shape into two balls. Sprinkle a little flour on dough and then flatten dough slightly. Press an unpeeled boiled egg into dough. Repeat for second ball of dough.

To make the crosses for the top of the bread, cut the ½ cup of dough that was set aside into four equally sized pieces. Roll and flatten them so that they are long enough to make a cross over dough. Place these dough strips over eggs and press into dough, making the shape of a cross.

Brush dough entirely with egg wash.

Bake for 15 minutes at 425 degrees F and then reduce heat to 375 degrees F for approximately another 15 minutes or until the bread is cooked. The bread is ready when it turns a golden brown color and makes a hollow sound when tapped.

Portuguese Bread Rolls / Papo Secos

Makes 18 to 24 bread rolls

1 (¼ ounce) dry active yeast packet
¼ cup lukewarm water
1 teaspoon sugar
4 pounds all-purpose flour, more for dusting

2 teaspoons salt
8 tablespoons olive oil
5 cups lukewarm water

....

Add yeast and sugar to warm water and mix vigorously until yeast is completely dissolved. Set aside for 10 minutes to form a yeast foam.

In a large bowl, combine flour and salt. Make a well in the center of flour, add yeast foam, olive oil and water, mixing slowly to form a dough.

Place dough on a flat surface and knead by hand for 10 minutes until dough is smooth and not too sticky. If dough is too wet, add a little more flour one tablespoon at a time.

Place kneaded dough in a bowl lightly dusted with flour. Cover with cloth and place in warm, draft-free location until dough doubles in size (approximately 1 hour).

When ready to bake the rolls, preheat oven to 350 degrees F.

On a lightly floured, flat surface, divide dough into approximately 24 sections and roll each into a ball, kneading each a little more. Flatten each ball with hand. Using a knife, slice an opening in the middle of each roll (without cutting all the way through). Place rolls on lightly floured baking trays, cover with a cloth and allow rolls to rise for another 15 minutes.

Place baking trays in the oven and cook until bread rolls are golden and sound hollow when tapped on the bottom (approximately 40 minutes).

Remove bread rolls from baking trays and place on a cooling rack.

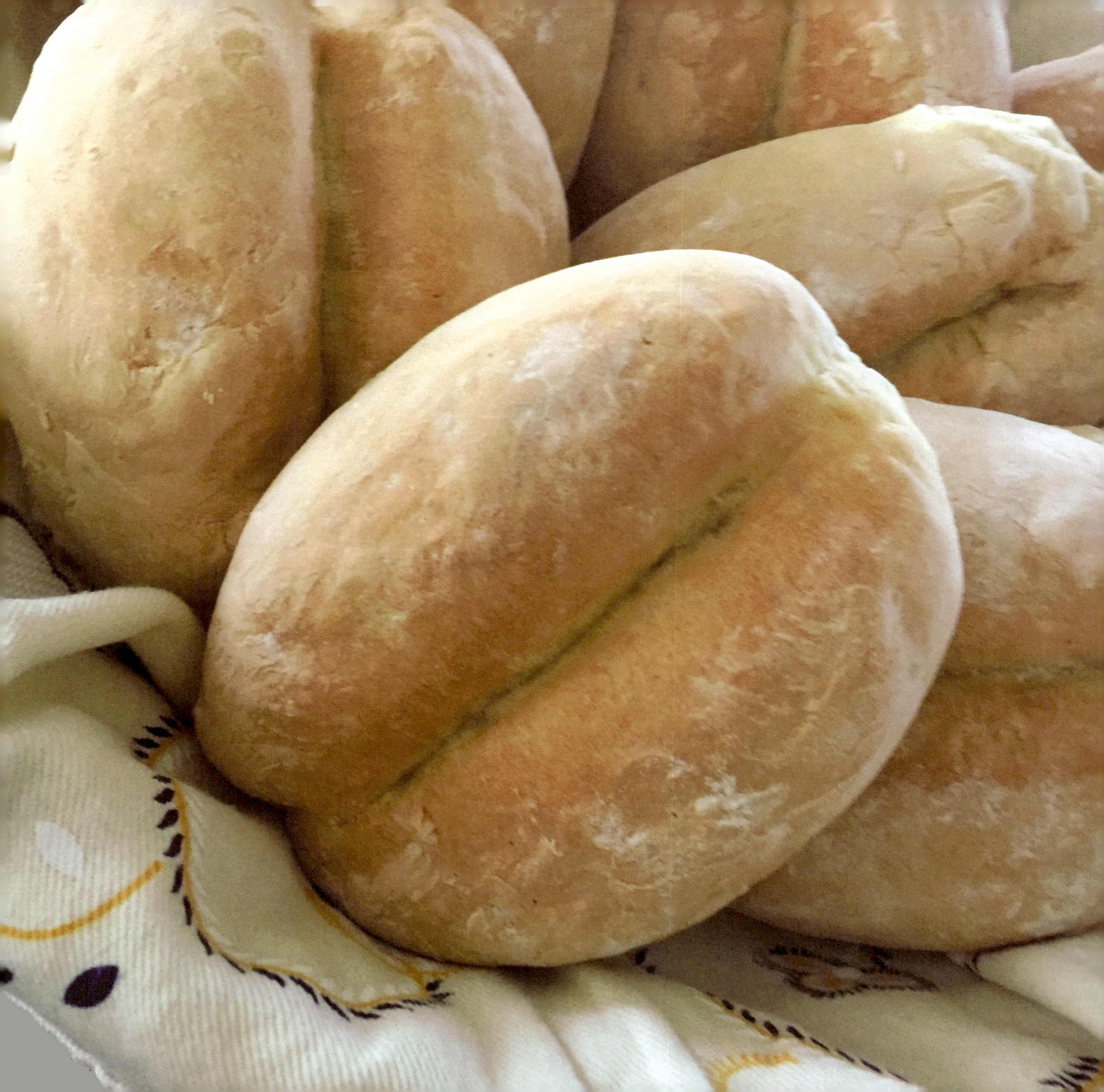

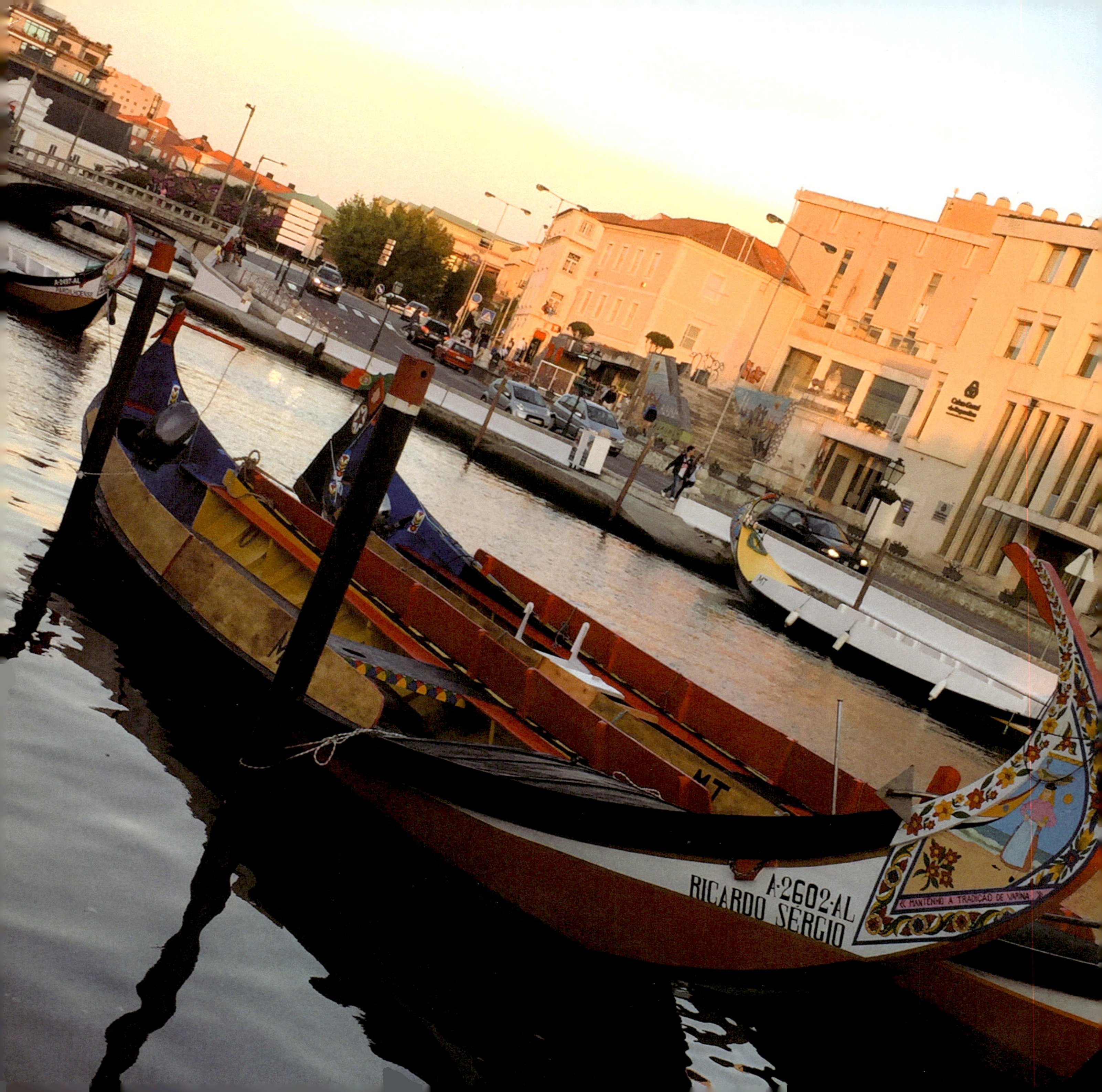
A·2602·AL
RICARDO SÉRGIO
« MANTENHO A TRADIÇÃO DE VARINA »
MT

My Favorite Portugal

My first trip to Portugal was at the age of one, and I've visited almost every summer since then. I also lived there for nine months after college, three of which I worked in Vila Nova de Gaia with a small view of the Douro River. For me, it was a dream come true to live in the Porto area. Over the years, I have been fortunate enough to travel throughout a good part of the country, but I still have much more left to see. Of all the places I visited to date in Portugal, here is a list of my Top 10 favorites. My number one has to be where my family came from, the place I have spent the most time and the place that every time I visit, I leave a little piece of myself behind.

1. **Figueira da Foz**: There is nowhere else in the world where I would rather have spent most of my summers. Figueira da Foz is where the mountains, the sun and the ocean meet. The town has a very cosmopolitan feel and is a place where I always felt safe, free and oh so content. In Figueira, the ocean is within walking distance and in view from almost anywhere you are. The town has an endless number of outdoor sidewalk cafes, playgrounds, restaurants and a very lively nightlife. All of these things make it the ideal place to rest, relax, recharge and have some fun for singles and families! Best of all, Figueira is where my family is from. If you visit this beautiful town, be sure to try a seafood dish such as Sardinhas Assadas (Grilled Sardines) or Polvo à Lagareiro (Octopus Lagareiro Style). Fresh seafood is abundant there. I also recommend trying the Migas from this region. They are absolutely delicious.

2. **Porto**: For me, it was love at first sight - the scenery, the sounds, the people and the food. Porto is the second largest city in Portugal, but somehow it still manages to feel quaint and so inviting. The city's beauty is unique and captivating beyond words. The locals are extremely friendly and accommodating. Also, many of the most recognized and popular Portuguese dishes originated there: Bacalhau à Gomes de Sá (Salted Cod Gomes de Sá Style), Francesinha (Layered Meat Sandwich with Sauce) and Tripas à Moda do Porto (Tripe and Bean Stew). I suggest you try all three!! There is something very extraordinary about this city, something that you have to experience to understand. Porto has a very special place in my heart and always will.

3. **Lisbon**: Portugal's capital city is just as gorgeous and romantic as any other old European city with its beautiful fountains, monuments, a castle on a hill and history. Lisbon is where I can have the one, the only Pastel de Belem, the mother of the Pastel de Nata, Portugal's most recognized pastry.

4. **Sintra**: When I think of Sintra, the words that pop into my head are, "there is just is no other place quite like Sintra". If you have ever been, you know exactly what I mean. Visiting this town is like walking into a fairytale with its beautiful palaces, castle on a hill and deep green enchanting forest. Sintra is the kind of place dreams are made of. I guarantee, if you visit, you will want to return again and again. While there, you must try the traditional pastry of the region, Travesseiros de Sintra.

5. **Obidos**: Visiting this castle-walled town is like stepping back into Medieval times. Viewing this town fully enclosed within castle walls from the outside while driving by on the roadside is spectacular. Walking through its streets and seeing the beautiful white houses trimmed with a pop of color and adorned with bright flowers is simply captivating. There is a special charm to this town. The feeling you get when visiting Obidos, is something that can't be described, but that must be experienced to fully understand. A visit to Obidos is not complete without a little Ginjinha in a chocolate cup.

6. **Evora**: The entire city is classified as a museum within itself, where the Romans once roamed, a place with lots of history and wonderful unique sites such as the Roman Temple of Evora and the Chapel of the Bones among them. Evora was once home to some of the most famous Portuguese, such as Vasco the Gama and Eça de Queiroz. While in the Alentejo region, I suggest visiting one of the wineries, such as Herdade de Esporão, to taste some of the best Portuguese wines.

7. **Lagos**: This town is a must for all beach lovers like myself. The beaches in Lagos take your breath away with their clear waters, beautiful cliffs and rock formations. One of my favorite shellfish is Conquilhas, which are typical of the Algarve and a must try. I also suggest trying the Morgados (Almond Cookies) while in the Algarve.

8. **The Interior Douro**: When you look at the vineyards from high atop the mountains here, you feel like you are very close to heaven. The view of the mountain ranges along the winding Douro River are like nothing I have ever seen before. Also, to see the vines that have been planted alongside some of the steepest mountains and near the edges of cliffs leaves you awestruck. The Douro is the perfect place to sample some Port Wine because this is the region where its grapes come from.

9. **Coimbra**: Ever since I was a child, I loved walking through the little winding streets of the downtown. Coimbra reminds of me of my younger days when I would take the train there and go shopping for a new pair of shoes to take back with me to America. I always liked to return to the U.S with a little "Euro" style. Also, it is home to one of the oldest universities in the world. On the way to Coimbra, you pass the oldest castle in Portugal in Montemor-o-Velho, which is a must visit. Also, on the way

to Coimbra, be sure to stop in Tentugal for the one and only Pastel de Tentugal served fresh out of the oven.

10. **Aveiro**. With its canals, Aveiro is considered the "Venice of Portugal". Here you can take a ride through the canals in the colorful "moliceiros" (canal boats). The brightly colored and striped beach houses in Costa Nova are unique and also quite a sight to see. This town is also home of the "Ovos Moles" (Sweetened Egg Yolks). I have fond memories of visiting Aveiro and coming home with a little wooden barrel filled with the Ovos Moles to enjoy.

Index

A
ALMOND TART 122

B
BAKED FISH WITH POTATOES 47
BEEF WITH ONIONS 60
BLACK EYED PEAS SALAD 96
BOILED DINNER 71
BRAZILIAN FLAN PUDDING 109

C
CABBAGE SOUP 22
CANNELLINI BEAN STEW 76
CHICKEN SOUP 26
CHICKEN STEW 68
CHICKEN STEW WITH PEAS AND POTATOES 69
CHOCOLATE MOUSSE 102
CHOCOLATE SALAME 104
CODFISH CAKES 4
CORNBREAD 126
CORNBREAD, BLACK EYED PEAS AND GREENS HASH 92

F
FARINHEIRA SAUSAGE WITH SCRAMBLED EGGS 13
FAVA BEAN STEW 78
FRESH CHEESE 6
FRIED SALTED COD WITH SAUTEED ONIONS 37

G
GREEN BEAN SOUP 28
GRILLED SARDINES 34

H
HEAVY CREAM & MARIA COOKIE LAYERED DESSERT 111
HOMEMADE FRENCH FRIES 94

L
LAYERED MARIA BISCUIT CAKE 107
LEEK SOUP 30
LIQUID CARAMEL 123
LITTLENECK CLAMS WITH GARLIC AND WINE SAUCE 2

M
MEAT BREAD 128
MERENGUE COOKIES 114
MERENGUE SOUFFLE 117
MONKFISH STEW 48

P
PINEAPPLE MOUSSE 110
PIRI PIRI CHICKEN 66
PORK RIBS 61
PORK SANDWICHES 62
PORTUGUESE BISCUITS 100
PORTUGUESE BREAD ROLLS 132
PORTUGUESE GREEN SOUP 18
PORTUGUESE KALE SOUP WITH BEANS 24
PORTUGUESE POPOVERS 112
PORTUGUESE STEAK WITH SAUCE 56
PORTUGUESE STYLE FRENCH TOAST 120
POT ROAST 58
PUNCHED POTATOES 84
PUREED RED KIDNEY BEAN SOUP 27
PUREED VEGETABLE SOUP 20

R

RED KIDNEY BEAN STEW 80
ROASTED PAPRIKA POTATOES 89
ROASTED PEPPER SALAD 97
ROASTED PORK LOIN 65

S

SALTED COD GOMES DE SA STYLE 38
SALTED COD LAGAREIRO STYLE 42
SALTED COD WITH EGGS AND FRIES 40
SALTED COD WITH HEAVY CREAM 43
SAUTEED KALE OR COLLARD GREENS 90
SEAFOOD MACARONI 50
SHRIMP MOZAMBIQUE 10
SIMPLE PORTUGUESE STEAK 54
SMALL FRIED SARDINES WITH ESCABECHE SAUCE 49
SPANISH-STYLE LITTLENECKS 8
SPICY ROASTED POTATOES 91
STEWED PEAS WITH POACHED EGGS 86
STEWED PORK CHOPS WITH POTATOES 64
STEWED SQUID WITH POTATOES 44
STEWED SQUID WITH RICE 46
SWEET ANGEL HAIR PASTA 119
SWEET PORTUGUESE EASTER BREAD 130
SWEET RICE 105

T

TEMPURA GREEN BEANS 14
TOMATO RICE 88
TUNA PATE 12
TWO MILK PUDDING WITH MERENGUE 116